The Sound of the Guns

MARQUIS DE GROUCHY, MARSHAL OF FRANCE

The Sound of the Guns
Marshal Grouchy and the Campaign of 1815—
an Anthology of Writings

Compiled by
Frederick Llewellyn

The Sound of the Guns
Marshal Grouchy and the Campaign of 1815—an Anthology of Writings
Compiled by Frederick Llewellyn

FIRST EDITION

Leonaur is an imprint of Oakpast Ltd
Copyright in this form © 2011 Oakpast Ltd

ISBN: 978-0-85706-613-8 (hardcover)
ISBN: 978-0-85706-614-5 (softcover)

http://www.leonaur.com

Publisher's Notes

The opinions of the authors represent a view of events in which he was a participant related from his own perspective, as such the text is relevant as an historical document.

The views expressed in this book are not necessarily those of the publisher.

Contents

Emmanuel de Grouchy—a Military Life	7
Concerning the Responsibility for the Loss of the Battle of Waterloo	16
Grouchy's Own Account of the Battle of Waterloo	17
Extracts From "The Campaign of 1815"	37
Particulars Regarding Marshal Grouchy's Army	100
Extract of a Letter from Marshal Ney to the Duke of Otranto, June 26, 1825	104
Extract from Remarks on General Gourgaud's Account of the Campaign of 1815	108
The Combats of Wavre and the Retreat of Grouchy	109
Notes and Comments	123
Marshal Grouchy's Report Addressed to the Emperor	132
Marshal Grouchy's Force	134

Emmanuel de Grouchy— a Military Life
by R. P. Dunn-Pattison

When the Revolution broke out in 1789 the young Count Emmanuel de Grouchy was serving as lieutenant-colonel in the Scotch company of the Gardes du Corps.

Born on October 23, 1766, the only son of the Marquis de Grouchy, the representative of an old Norman family which could trace its descent from before the days of William the Conqueror, Emmanuel de Grouchy had entered the army at the age of fourteen. After a year's service in the marine artillery he had been transferred to a cavalry regiment of the line, and on his twentieth birthday had been selected for the Gardes du Corps.

A keen student of military history and devoted to his profession, the young Count had read widely and thought much. Impressionable and enthusiastic, a philosophical liberal by nature, he eagerly absorbed the teaching of the Encyclopaedists. As events developed, he found that his position in the Gardes du Corps was antagonistic to his principles, and, at his own request, at the end of 1791 he was transferred to the Twelfth regiment of *Chasseurs* as lieutenant-colonel commanding. After a few months' service with this regiment he was promoted brigadier-general, and served successively under General Montesquieu with the Army of the Midi, and under Kellermann with the Army of the Alps.

At the commencement of 1793, while on leave in Normandy, he was hurriedly despatched to the west to take part in the civil war in La Vendée. No longer Comte de Grouchy but plain Citizen-General Grouchy, for the next three years he saw almost continuous service in the civil war, with the exception of a few months when, like all *ci-devant* nobles, he was dismissed the service by the decree of the incompetent Bouchotte. But Clanclaux, who commanded the Army of La Vendée, had found in him a most useful subordinate and a sound adviser; and accordingly, at his instance, the *ci-devant* noble was restored to his rank, and sent back as chief of the staff to the Army of the West, and in April, 1795, promoted general of division. Clear-headed, firmly convinced of the soundness of his opinions, without being bigoted or revengeful, Grouchy saw that the cruel methods of many of the generals did more to continue the war than the political tenets of the Vendéens and Chouans, and he used his influence with Clanclaux, and later with Hoche, to restrain useless reprisals and crush the rebellion by overwhelming the armed forces of the rebels, not by insulting women and shooting prisoners. The problem to be solved was a difficult one, as he pointed out in a memoir written for Clanclaux.

It is the population of the entire country which is on your hands, a population which suddenly rushes together to fight, if it is strong enough to crush you; which hurls itself against your flanks and rear, and then as suddenly disappears, when not strong enough to resist you.

His solution of the difficulty was to wear down resistance by light mobile columns, and to starve the enemy out by devastating the country.

In September, 1795, on Clanclaux's retirement, the commissioners attached to the Army of the West wished to invest Grouchy with the command, but the general refused the post; for, clear counsellor and good adviser as he was, he lacked self-confidence, and knew that he was not fit for the position. It was this horror of undertaking responsibility which dragged him down during all his career, and which, on the two occasions when fortune gave him his chance to rise, made him choose the safe but inglorious road of humdrum mediocrity. In 1796 came his first chance: after a brief period of service with the Army of the North in Holland he was once again at his old work under Hoche in the west, when the Directory determined to try to retaliate for the English participation in the Chouan revolt by raising a hornet's nest in Ireland. At the end of December a force of fifteen thousand men under Hoche, with Grouchy as second in command, set sail for Ireland.

Unfortunately the expedition met with bad weather, the ship on which Hoche sailed got separated from the rest of the fleet, and, when Grouchy arrived at the rendezvous in Bantry Bay, he found the greater part of the expedition, but no general-in-chief. In spite of this he rightly determined to effect a landing, but had not the necessary force of character to ensure his orders being carried out, and after six days' procrastination Admiral Bouvet, pleading heavy weather, refused to allow his ships to remain off the coast, and the expedition returned to France. If Grouchy had been able to get his orders obeyed, all would have been well, for on the very day after his squadron left Bantry Bay, Hoche himself arrived at the rendezvous. As Grouchy said, if he had only flung that—Admiral Bouvet into the sea all would have been right. Where Grouchy hesitated and failed a Napoleon would have acted and conquered.

Hoche died, and Grouchy, who under his influence had disapproved of the policy of France towards the Italian States, at once accepted employment in Italy. He soon had to rue his decision, for he found himself entrusted with the task of using underhand means to drive the king of Sardinia from his country. Still, he obeyed his orders to the letter. During negotiations he secretly introduced French troops into the citadel at Turin and then seized the fortresses of Novara, Alessandria, and Chiasso. Meanwhile he terrified the unfortunate monarch by announcing the arrival of imaginary columns of troops, suborned the king's Council, and so worked on the feelings of the bewildered sovereign that he escaped by night from his palace and fled across the sea. But though their king had deserted them, the Piedmontese did not tamely submit, and for the next few months the general was busy tracking out and capturing the numerous members of the secret societies who were avenging their country by cutting the throats of Frenchmen.

While striking with a heavy hand at these conspirators, Grouchy was level-headed enough to understand that the proper method of tackling the problem was to remove the grievance. In his opinion it was not the people so much as the Church which was opposed to the French, and accordingly he did his best to get Joubert to issue a proclamation that there should be no interference with religion.

Still, the situation must have been galling to a man of culture and a theoretical liberal, for, while forcing democratic institutions on an unwilling people, he had at the same time to strip their capital of all objects of art; and while issuing proclamations for the freedom of religion he had to arrange for the passage of the Pope on his way to captivity. In May, 1799, the general was recalled from his governorship of Turin, for the Austrians and Russians were invading Lombardy and

Joubert was concentrating his forces. The campaign, as far as Grouchy was concerned, was short, for while attempting to stem the flight of the left wing after the battle of Novi he was ridden over and captured by the Allies. Four sabre cuts, one bullet wound, and several bayonet thrusts kept him in hospital for some time; when he was well enough to be moved he was sent to Grätz, and it was not till a year later—in June, 1800—that his exchange was effected. But he soon had his revenge on the Austrians, for in the autumn he was despatched to join the army under Moreau, which was operating on the Danube, and arrived at headquarters in time to take part in the battle of Hohenlinden. In the face of a blinding snowstorm Grouchy's division drove back the main column of the enemy, and after hours of murderous hand-to-hand fighting in the forest, he shared with Ney the honour of the last charge which drove the enemy in hopeless rout.

It was on his return from Hohenlinden that the ex-Count met Bonaparte. The First Consul, who aimed at conciliating the old nobility, made much of him, employed him on a confidential mission to Italy, and nominated him inspector-general of cavalry. This post admirably suited Grouchy, who was a horseman by nature and a cavalry soldier by instinct. Later, on the formation of the Army of the Ocean, he was appointed to the command of an infantry division in Marmont's corps in Holland, and it was with Marmont that he made the campaign of 1805. In October, 1806, he was summoned from Italy to a more important command. The Grand Army was advancing on Prussia, and Napoleon had need of capable leaders to command his vast masses of cavalry. Grouchy was entrusted with the second division of dragoons of the cavalry corps under Murat and played a prominent part in the battle of Prinzlow and the pursuit to Lübeck.

At Eylau he had a narrow escape: his charger was killed in the middle of the melee and he was only saved by the devotion of his *aide-de-camp*; though much shaken, he was able to resume command of his division, and distinguished himself by his fierce charges in the blinding snow. At Friedland a chance occurred for which his capacity proved fully equal. Murat was absent at Königsberg trying to get across the enemy's rear, and Grouchy was in command of all the reserve cavalry at the moment the advance guard interrupted the Russian retreat. It was his admirable handling of the cavalry under Lannes's directions which held the Russians in check for sixteen hours, until Napoleon was able to concentrate his divisions and give the Russians the *coup-de-grâce*. The emperor showed his gratitude by presenting the general with the Grand Cross of Baden, investing him with the Cordon of the Legion of Honour, and granting him the domain of Nowawies, in the department of Posen.

The following year, 1808, saw Grouchy, now a Count of the Empire, with Murat in Spain, acting as governor of Madrid. But when, in the autumn, Joseph evacuated all the western provinces, Grouchy, whose health had been much shaken by the Polish campaign, was granted leave of absence and took care not to be sent back, for he had seen enough of the Spanish to foresee the terrible difficulties of guerrilla warfare; moreover, the annexation of the country was contrary to his ideas of political justice. When the war with Austria was imminent Napoleon sent him to Italy to command the cavalry of the viceroy's army. With Prince Eugène he fought through Styria and Carinthia and distinguished himself greatly at the Battle of Raab. At Wagram his cavalry was attached to Davout's corps, and his fierce charges, which helped to break the Austrian left, brought him again under the notice of the emperor, who showed his appreciation by appointing him colonel-general of *chasseurs*.

In 1812 the Count was summoned once again to the field, to command the third corps of reserve cavalry with the Grand Army in Russia. At Moskowa his *cuirassiers*, sabre in hand, drove the Russians out of the great redoubt, but Grouchy himself was seriously wounded. During the retreat from Moscow he commanded one of the "Sacred Bands" of officers who personally guarded the emperor, but his health, never good, completely broke down under the strain and he was allowed to return straight home from Vilna. A year elapsed before he had sufficiently recovered to take the field, and it was not till the beginning of 1814 that he was fit for service. During the campaign in France, first under Victor and later with Marmont, he commanded the remnant of the reserve cavalry; but on March 7th at Craonne he was once again so badly wounded that he had to throw up his command.

During the Restoration Grouchy remained at his home; his relations with the Bourbons were not cordial, and he bitterly resented the loss of his title of colonel-general of *chasseurs*. Accordingly, when Napoleon returned from Elba and France seemed to welcome him with open arms, in spite of having accepted the Cross of St. Louis, he had no scruple in answering the emperor's summons. He was entrusted with the operations against the Duc d'Angoulême round Lyons, but disliked the task, for he remembered the fate of the Duc d'Enghien, and in spite of Napoleon's protests that he only desired to capture the Duke in order to make the Austrians send back the Empress, Grouchy determined that, if possible, while doing everything to defeat the royalists, he would not capture d'Angoulême. Unfortunately, the Duke refused the opportunity to escape which was offered him, and Grouchy had to make him a prisoner. However, Napoleon, anxious to stand well with the Powers of Europe, at once ordered him to be set free. At the same time he sent Grouchy to command the Army of the Alps, giving him his Marshal's baton. The new Marshal was delighted with his promotion; he had now served for twenty years as general of division, and although only forty-nine, had practically given up all hope of promotion. But scarcely had he reached his new command when he was recalled to Paris.

With Murat in disgrace and Bessières dead, the emperor had no great cavalry leader on whom he could rely, and, remembering the new Marshal's exploits at Friedland and Wagram, and his staunchness in 1814, he determined to entrust him with the command of the reserve cavalry. Unfortunately for Napoleon and Grouchy, the exigencies of the campaign forced the emperor to divide his army; so, while entrusting Ney with a part of his troops, with orders to pursue the English, and keeping the Guard and reserves under his immediate control, he gave Grouchy the command of two corps of infantry and one of cavalry; in all, some thirty-three thousand men.

The appointment was an unfortunate one, for the marshal, though in many respects a good cavalry leader, had never before had the command of a large body of mixed troops, and even his cavalry successes had been obtained when under the orders of a superior: at Friedland he was under Lannes; at Wagram under Davout; at Moskowa under Eugène; and in 1814 under either Victor or Marmont. But what was most unfortunate about the selection was that Grouchy had not enough personal authority to enforce his orders on his corps commanders, and the fiery Vandamme not only despised but hated him because he had received the baton which he hoped was to have been his, while Girard was a personal enemy.

At Ligny, where Napoleon himself supervised the attack, all went well, but from the moment fighting ceased difficulties began. Immediately after the battle the emperor entrusted the marshal with the pursuit of the Prussians, but Pajol, who commanded his light cavalry, carried out his reconnaissance in a perfunctory manner, and reported that the Prussians had retreated towards Namur. Grouchy received this news at 4 a.m. on June 17th, but he did not dare to disturb the emperor's rest, and it was 8 a.m. before he could see him and demand detailed orders. Napoleon, trusting to Pajol's report, thought that the Prussians were absolutely demoralised and were leaving the theatre of war, and so he kept the marshal talking about Paris and politics till 11 a.m. Consequently it was 11.30 before he received exact orders, penned by Bertrand, which told him to proceed to Gembloux, keeping his forces concentrated; to reconnoitre the different roads leading to Namur and Maestricht, and to inform the emperor of the Prussians' intentions, adding, "It is important to know what Blücher and Wellington mean to do, and whether they prefer to unite their armies in order to cover Brussels and Liège, by trying their fortunes in another battle."

Bad staff directions and heavy rains retarded the advance, and it took six hours for the troops to cover the nine miles to Gembloux, where at eight in the evening Grouchy heard that part of the Prussians had fallen back on Wavre, which meant that they might still unite with the English to cover Brussels. He at once reported this to the emperor, adding that Blücher had retired on Liège and the artillery on Namur. But, in spite of the fact that on the evening of the seventeenth Napoleon knew that this was a mistake, and that the Prussians were actually massed round Wavre, it was not till 10 a.m. on the morning of Waterloo that he sent to the marshal informing him of the Prussians' concentration, and telling him that "he must therefore move thither (*i.e.*, to Wavre) in order to approach us, and to push before him any Prussians who may have stopped at Wavre."

This was the exact course which Grouchy had determined to pursue. It is therefore quite clear that neither the emperor nor the marshal had dreamed that Blücher would attempt to give any assistance to the English in their position at Waterloo. At 11 a.m., when his columns were just approaching Wavre, the marshal heard the commencement of the cannonade at Waterloo. Girard entreated him to march to the sound of the cannon, but Grouchy had what he considered distinct orders to pursue the Prussians; he was now in touch with them, and with a force of thirty-three thousand men he did not dare to make a flank march in the face of what, he was becoming convinced, was the whole Prussian army. At 5 p.m. he received Napoleon's despatch, hastily written at 1 p.m., ordering him to turn westward and crush the Prussian corps which was marching on the emperor's right rear, but by then his main force was heavily engaged at Wavre, and even if he had been able to despatch part of his force it could not have arrived at

Mont St. Jean till long after the end of the battle.

On the morning of the nineteenth the marshal was preparing to pursue Thielmann's corps, which, on the previous evening, he had driven from Wavre, when he heard of the catastrophe at Waterloo. He immediately stopped the pursuit, and, by rapid marching, reached Namur before the Allies could cut him off, and, by a skilful retreat, brought back his thirty-three thousand men to Paris before the enemy arrived at the gates. But instead of the thanks he had expected he found himself saddled with the blame of the loss of Waterloo. The disaster, however, clearly rested on the emperor, whose orders were vague, and who had not realised the extraordinary moral courage of Blücher and the stubbornness of the Prussians, and if Napoleon did not foresee this he could not blame Grouchy for being equally blind.

The marshal did all that a mediocre man could do. He carefully carried out the orders given him, trusting, no doubt, too much to the letter, too little to the spirit. But long years spent in a subordinate position under a military hierarchy like that of the Empire were bound to stifle all initiative, and it was not to be supposed that the man who, twenty years earlier, had failed to rise to the occasion in Ireland would, after at last gaining his Marshal's baton, risk his reputation by marching, like Desaix at Marengo, to the sound of the guns, across the front of an enemy vastly superior to himself, through a difficult country partially waterlogged and intercepted by deep broad streams, contrary to what seemed his definite orders.

The marshal's career really ended on the abdication of the emperor, though he was appointed by the Provisional government to the command of the remains of the Army of the North, and in this capacity proclaimed the emperor's son as Napoleon II. On gaining Paris he found himself subordinate to Davout, an old enemy. Accordingly he threw up his command and retired into private life. After his conduct during the Hundred Days he could expect no mercy from the returned Bourbons, and was glad to escape abroad. Included in the general pardon, he returned to France in 1818, but his marshalate was annulled, and he never regained his baton, though on the accession of Charles X. he was actually received at court.

But though the king might forgive, his favourites and ministers could not forget, and in December, 1824, he was included among the fifty generals of Napoleon who were placed on the retired list, an action which General Foy shrewdly remarked was "a cannon-shot charged at Waterloo, fired ten years after the battle, and pointed direct at its mark." Like many another of the marshals, the veteran retained his health and faculties for many years, and defended his character and actions and criticised his enemies with the same clear logic which had so powerfully contributed to his early advancement; for the ex-Marshal wielded the pen as easily as the sword. It was not till 1847 that death carried off the sturdy old warrior at the age of eighty-one.

Concerning the Responsibility for the Loss of the Battle of Waterloo

The following is an explanatory excerpt from a letter to Mr. Bixby from the dealer through whom Marschal Grouchy's MS. account of the Battle of Waterloo was obtained:

> When I purchased the manuscript now in your possession I was assured that it was an article written by Grouchy, sent to a magazine editor, but for some reason never published. My research of yesterday leads me to believe that, instead of being an unpublished article, it is the *original manuscript of the very account* on which centres the entire literature concerning who lost the Battle of Waterloo... The manuscript would thus prove to be far more valuable than I had at first supposed, as the central document in an historical controversy extending over half a century concerning the greatest historical event of that century.

Grouchy's account follows immediately hereafter.

Grouchy's Own Account of the Battle of Waterloo

A corner of the curtain covering the causes for the loss of the Battle of Waterloo lifted—the impossibility on account of its position for the army corps under the orders of Marshal Grouchy to take part in this battle

The four days' campaign which ended the military career of Napoleon opened on the 15th day of June, 1815. The French army, 110,000 men strong, crossed the Sambre at Charleroy and engaged with a body of 20,000 Prussians which had taken position behind that city in order to retard the Emperor's advance. Some troops of the enemy which occupied Charleroy having retired toward Bruxelles by Quatre Bras, Marshal Ney was despatched by this route with 40,000 men. Immediately after the passage of the Sambre, the Emperor having with him Marshal Grouchy and the rest of the army, making 70,000 men, moved toward Fleurus, and on the 16th of June attacked the main Prussian army, which he had hoped to surprise while encamped, but which he found drawn up in the plains behind that city.

Although judged to be about 100,000 strong, it was defeated after offering a stubborn resistance. Toward ten o'clock in the evening Marshal Blucher, profiting by the obscurity of the night, effected his retreat, presumably in the direction of Namur and Wavre where, as was afterwards learned, lay the army of General Bülow, who was not able to arrive in time to take part in the battle of the 16th. (I say presumably, for cannons and prisoners were taken on both of these routes.)

Up to half-past twelve at noon on the 17th of June the Emperor—who until then had ordered no movement of the army—was waiting a report from Marshal Ney; as soon as he received it, he ordered Marshal Grouchy to take his place at the head of the corps of infantry under Generals Vendame and Gerard, and of the cavalry under Generals Pajol and Excelmans, forming a total of some thirty thousand men, and to follow the Prussian army; this in spite of the fact that he had been informed that it had fifteen hours' start of the army sent to pursue it, having effected its retreat the evening before at ten o'clock, and the few light cavalry troops which had followed it had not been able to retard its movement.

Napoleon, marching to the left with his guard and the other troops that had fought at Fleurus, went to join Marshal Ney, who on the 16th had defeated the advance guard of the Duke of Wellington near Quatre Bras. He then found himself facing the entire English and Belgian army. Marshal Ney on the 16th would have destroyed the advance guard which he had been fighting, if, at the moment when the engagement was at its height, he had not been deprived of the regiments of the Count d'Erlon, nearly 20,000 strong. These troops spent the day in lazily covering the distance between Fleurus and Quatre Bras; they did not fire a single gun, and were of no use to the army fighting at Fleurus, where they did not even arrive!

The only orders given by the Emperor to Marshal Grouchy after he was sent off on the 17th, and the day of the Battle of Waterloo on the 18th, are those enclosed in a letter of the Marshal, Duke of Dalmatie (Major-General Soult), written on the field of the Battle of Waterloo the 18th at one o'clock in the afternoon and delivered at four o'clock to Marshal Grouchy, then fighting with the Prussians, whose rear guard he had captured at eleven o'clock in the morning, one league from Wavre. After having been overthrown it was rallied in that city by the army of Marshal Blucher, who, since the evening before had taken its position on the heights behind the Dyle.

Toward one o'clock Marshal Grouchy ordered General Vendame to take by main force the bridge over the Dyle. This attack not succeeding, he directed General Gerard and the cavalry of General Pajol to take the mill of Bielge and the village of Limellette, in order to effect there the passage of the river, while General Vendame kept up the combat in Wavre, and while a false attack was being carried on at the expense of that city.

Such was the state of affairs on the arrival of the officers bringing the dispatch from the Duke of Dalmatie, the tenor of which is here given over the next page:[1]

---

1. The French dispatch in French is included, along with others, at the end of the next part of this book in the extract from *The Campaign of 1815*.

Battle of Waterloo handed to me by my friend Grouchy (Marshal) with a request that I would translate it for the National Intelligencer

Aug. 20th 1818

THE ABOVE INDORSEMENT APPEARS ON THE BACK OF THE GROUCHY MS.

The 18th, one o'clock, p. m.

To Marshal Grouchy:

Monsieur le Maréchale, you wrote this morning at six o'clock to the Emperor that you would march upon Sarra Valain; then your project was to go to Corbaix and to Wavre. This movement is in accordance with His Majesty's orders, which were communicated to you. The Emperor, however, commanded me to tell you that you must keep manoeuvring in our direction. It is your duty to see how we stand, in order to act accordingly and to join forces with us, so that you may always be ready to engage and crush whatever troops of the enemy may attempt to disturb our right wing.

At this moment the battle on the Waterloo side is already won; the enemy's centre is at Mont St. Jean; so do your best to join our right.

   (Signed) Le Duc de Dalmatie.

P. S. A letter which has just been intercepted brings the news that General Bülow is to attack our right flank. We think we see his regiment on the heights of St. Lambert; so do not therefore lose an instant in coming and joining us and in crushing Bülow, whom you will take *in flagrante delictu*.

   (Signed) Le Marshal Duc de Dalmatie.

As the Prussians were masters of the most practicable communication between Wavre and Waterloo, and as there was no direct route between Waterloo and the position near Wavre, where the troops under Marshal Grouchy's orders were fighting, they were obliged, in order to join the Emperor, to travel over nearly five leagues and to cross a difficult wooded country, cut by ravines.

The orders to join forces were sent at one o'clock, p. m., and did not arrive until four o'clock. Marshal Grouchy's troops, which had to force the passage of the river, were then fighting with an enemy superior in numbers and occupying a strong position, which it was necessary to capture. It was then physically impossible for them to arrive at Waterloo in time to change the fortune of the day, which was decided—as all those instructed in military affairs well knew—at the moment when General Bülow's troops appeared on the flank of the French army: in other words, at the moment when Napoleon summoned Marshal Grouchy to him.

In examining with some attention the letter of Marshal Duc de

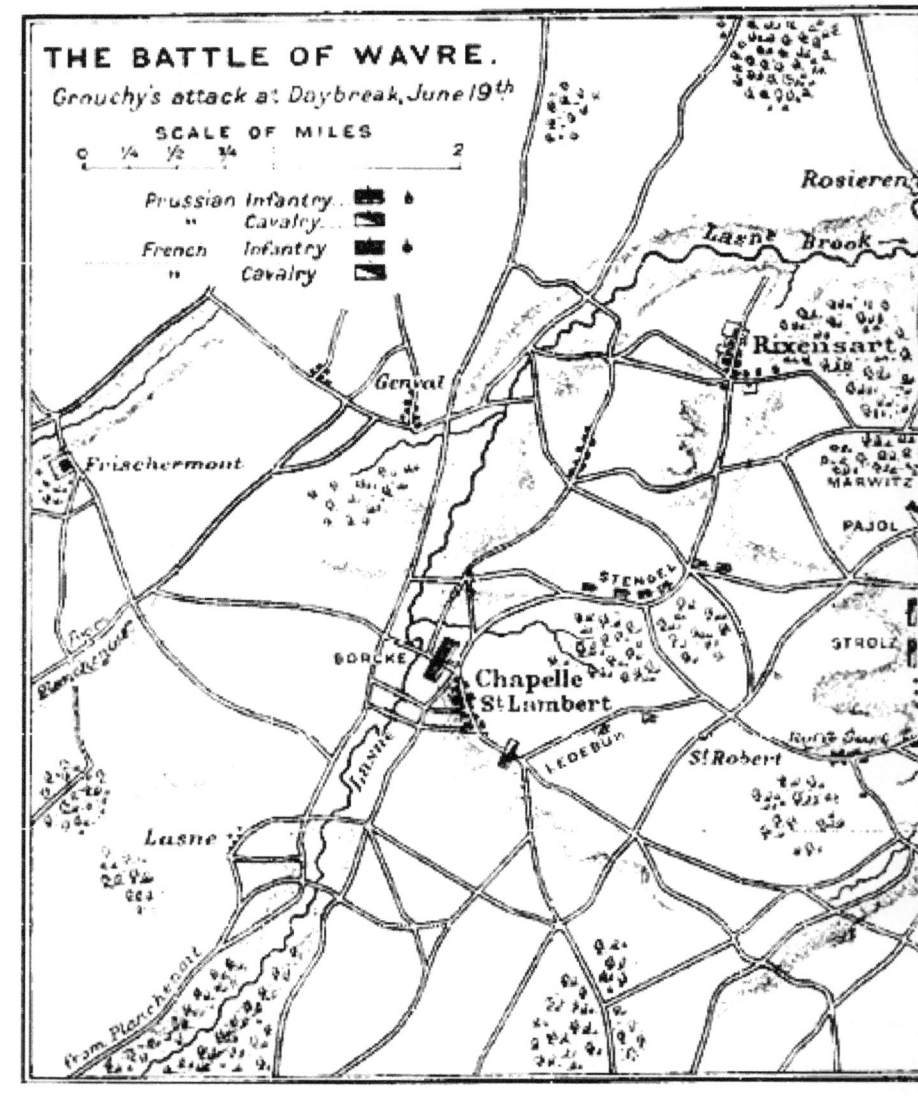

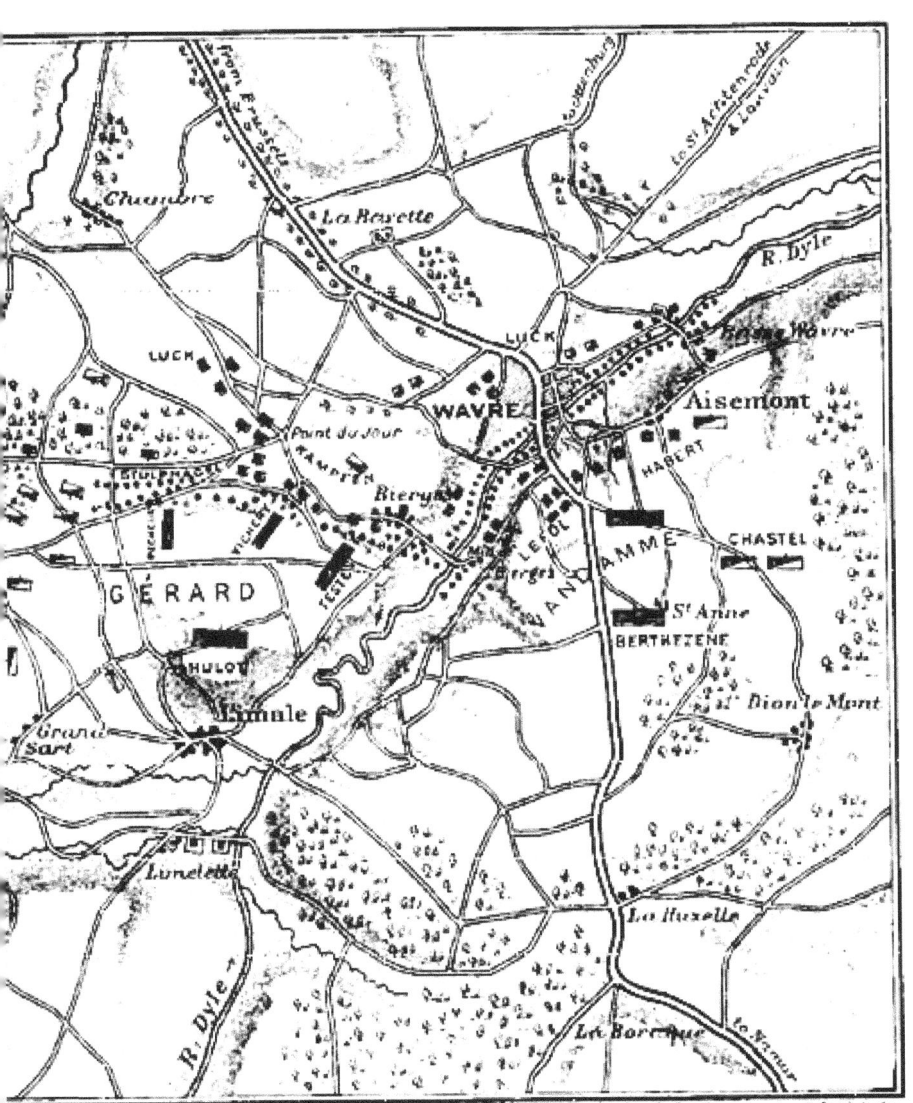

Dalmatie, one is convinced,—

> 1st. That Marshal Grouchy operated according to the Emperor's intentions in marching upon Wavre.
>
> 2nd. That Napoleon did not think of summoning this Marshal until one o'clock in the afternoon, at the very instant when the head of General Bülow's column showed itself on the Heights of St. Lambert, and consequently when it was much too late to paralyze the flank attack of the Prussians.

Finally, it is well to remember what English pride and Prussian boasting have taken great care to minimize—I mean the numerical superiority of the allies. It was so great that in spite of Marshal Blucher's losses at Fleurus, his army, united since the 17th with Bülow's troops at Wavre, was triple the force under Marshal Grouchy's command sent to pursue him. The pursuit could not give great results, because it was not ordered until fifteen hours after Blucher's retreat. He had the time to rally his army, to place it advantageously, and he did not expose himself or make a great display of genius in directing half of his army on Napoleon's flank, while with the other half he would retard for some time the march of Marshal Grouchy; would dispute with him the passage of the Dyle and (on account of the forces which he left before him and of their position) would have even chances of crushing his contingent.

Only a blind and even culpable partiality (for such it is when an attempt is made to obscure the historic truth and to betray the sound opinion, which evidence of facts, experience of war, and military methods have necessarily inculcated) could possibly claim, as did the judicious author of the *Considérations sur l'Art de la Guerre*, that Marshal Grouchy's troops remained on the 18th in stupid immobility and that on hearing the cannon on his left he ought to have disregarded the instructions which had been given him, to have abandoned the pursuit of Marshal Blucher, and to have gone to join Napoleon.

The writers of articles inserted in the different papers are equally mistaken when they declare that Marshal Grouchy was deluded by Marshal Blucher; that he took the troops left before him for the main Prussian army and that if he had followed a parallel march, contrary to his orders, which were to pursue Marshal Blucher and to complete his defeat by attacking him wherever he happened to fall in with him, it would have saved Napoleon.

Without doubt this assertion would have been justified, if on the evening of the 17th Napoleon had sent to Marshal Grouchy orders to join forces with him. Or even if on the 18th at daybreak these orders had come, then they might have been carried out, at a profitable time, and probably the fate of the battle and the issue of the campaign would have been different; but in truth, given as they were, on the 18th at one o'clock in the afternoon to troops who could not receive them until many hours after, who had the passage of a river to effect, and nearly five hours of marching in order to get there, and given only when the head of the Prussian column was in sight, it became illusive; for it was obviously impossible that the cooperation of Marshal Grouchy could have taken place, and that he prevented the honours of the victory from falling into the hands of the French army, which did not cease to reap a harvest of them at the field of Waterloo, until the moment of the flank attack of the Prussians.

N. B. The original of the orders of the Marshal Duke of Dalmatie and all the official documents relating to this campaign are in the hands of a public officer at Paris and will be published some day. Not being supported by substantial evidence the history of this campaign and of the causes of this disaster would be only a sort of declaration bearing the colours of the party to which its writer now belongs.

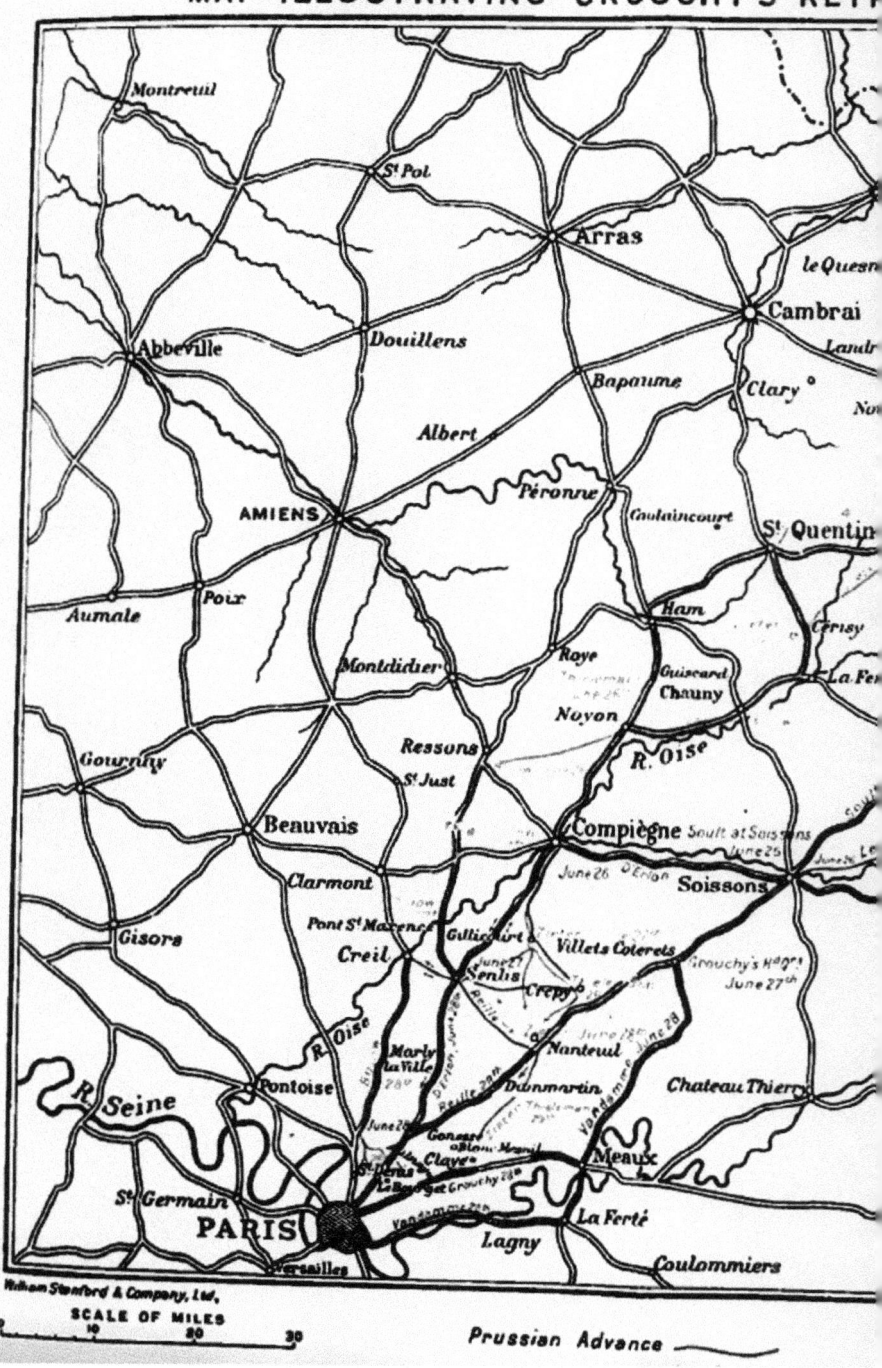

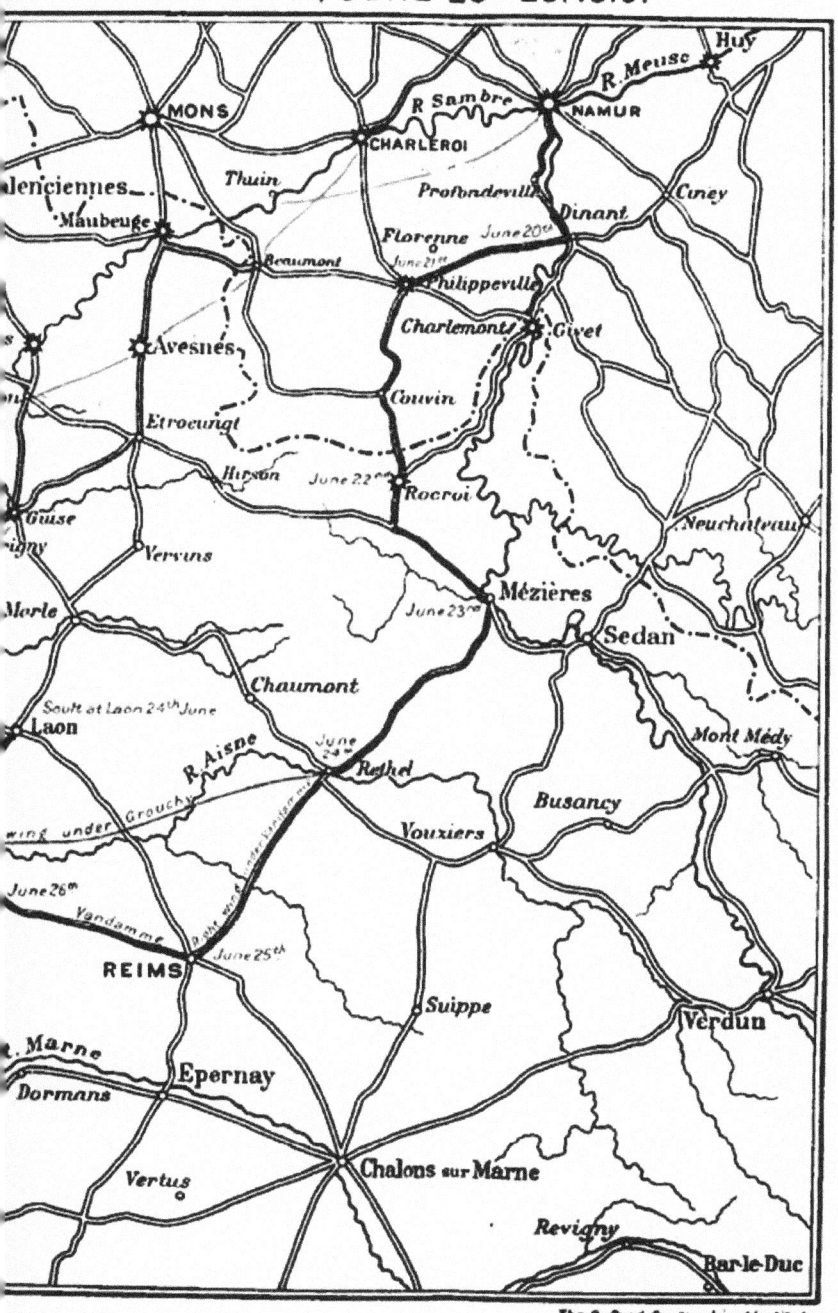

AT FROM NAMUR, JUNE 20-28, 1815.

French Retreat

retard par la pluie, a dix heures du soir, et le feu de l'artillerie (après qui l'a fait suivre) majent par été dans le cas de s'arrêter son mouvement).

Napoléon marchant ;—

L'arrivée de l'officier porteur de la dépêche de Duc de Dalmatie n'est venu la tenir ; le 18. a une heure après Midi.

Au nom de Pronsby —

" Monsieur le Maréchal, vous avez écrit de Matoa à six heures à l'Empereur, que vous Marcherier sur Sarragalain). Donc votre projet était de vous porter à retraite) vers la Sulbe, à dix heures du soir, et la rue de Castalais (ordre qui n'a pas été suivi, ayant passé par les dans le bois de (Becker sous Mouzement))

Napoléon marchant pour sa gauche avec sa garde, et les autres troupes qui arrivent (Combattit à Fleurus, alla joindre le Maréchal Ney qui le 16 avait défait l'avant garde du duc de Wellington près des quatre bras, et qui se trouvait alors, en présence de toute l'armée anglaise, et Belge. (Le Maréchal Ney eut, avant-hier le 16, l'avant garde qu'il avait combattu) si au moment de l'engagement était le plus vif, on ne lui eut retiré le corps du comte D'Erlon, fort de vingt mil hommes, qui passa la journée en promenades inutiles entre Fleurus et les quatre bras, ne serait pour une armée et il fut avenu utile à l'armée qui le battit à Ruissignou et Marroy même Jours)

les ordres adres- sons donnés par l'empereur au Maréchal Grouchy, depuis qu'il l'été détaché le 17. et le jour de la bataille de Waterloo le 18. sont aux renfermées dans une lettre du Maréchal Duc de Dalmatie (Soult), major général, écrite du champ de

bataille de Waterloo, le 18 a une heure après midi, et remise à quelque heures la
soir au Maréchal Grouchy, après avoir passé à être les prisonniers dont il avoit
atteint l'arrière) – Que le Maréchal [...] – [...] [...] [...] [...] [...] [...] [...] [...] [...] après avoir
été culbutée, elle s'étoit rallié dans Wavre à l'armée du Maréchal Blücher, qui de
la veille y avoit pris position sur les hauteurs en arrière de la Dyle; qui là,
partagée. Vers les une heure, le Maréchal Grouchy ayant chargé le général
Vandamme Berleton de passer sur le pont sur la Dyle, son attaque n'a suffisant pas
il avoit dirigé le général Gérard et la Cavalerie du général Vapol, sur le moulin
de Bielge et le village de Limelette pour y effectuer le passage de la rivière tandis
que le général Vandamme continuerait le combat dans Wavre, et quoiqu'après
attaques s'exposaient aux abords de Wavre.

Et tout l'état des choses lorsque
l'arrivée de l'officier porteur de la dépêche du Duc de Dalmatie est venu la trouver,
à 18. à une heure après Midi.

Au nom du Prince,
"Monsieur le Maréchal, vous avez écrit Etats à l'Empereur
que vous marcheriez sur Sart-à-Wavre. Donc votre projet était de vous porter à

MAP ILLUSTATING THE OPERATIONS

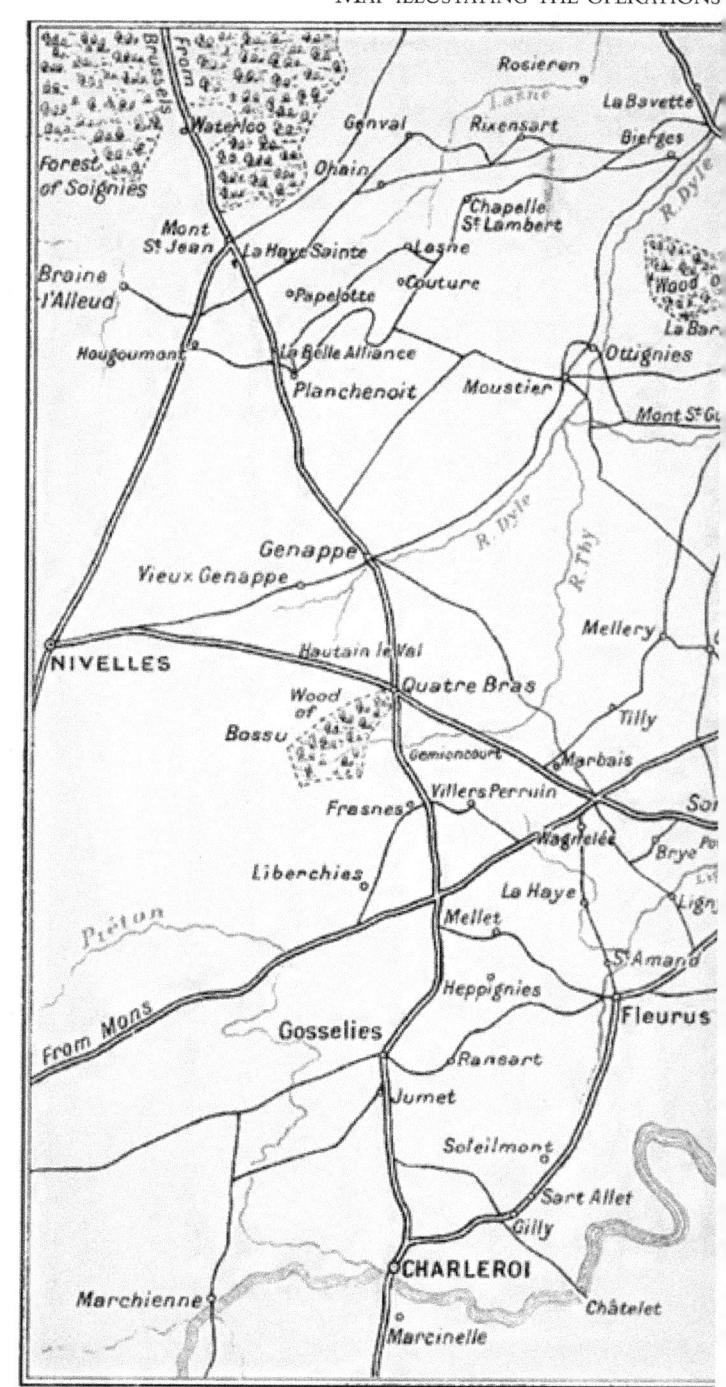

OF JUNE 15TH TO 20TH 1815

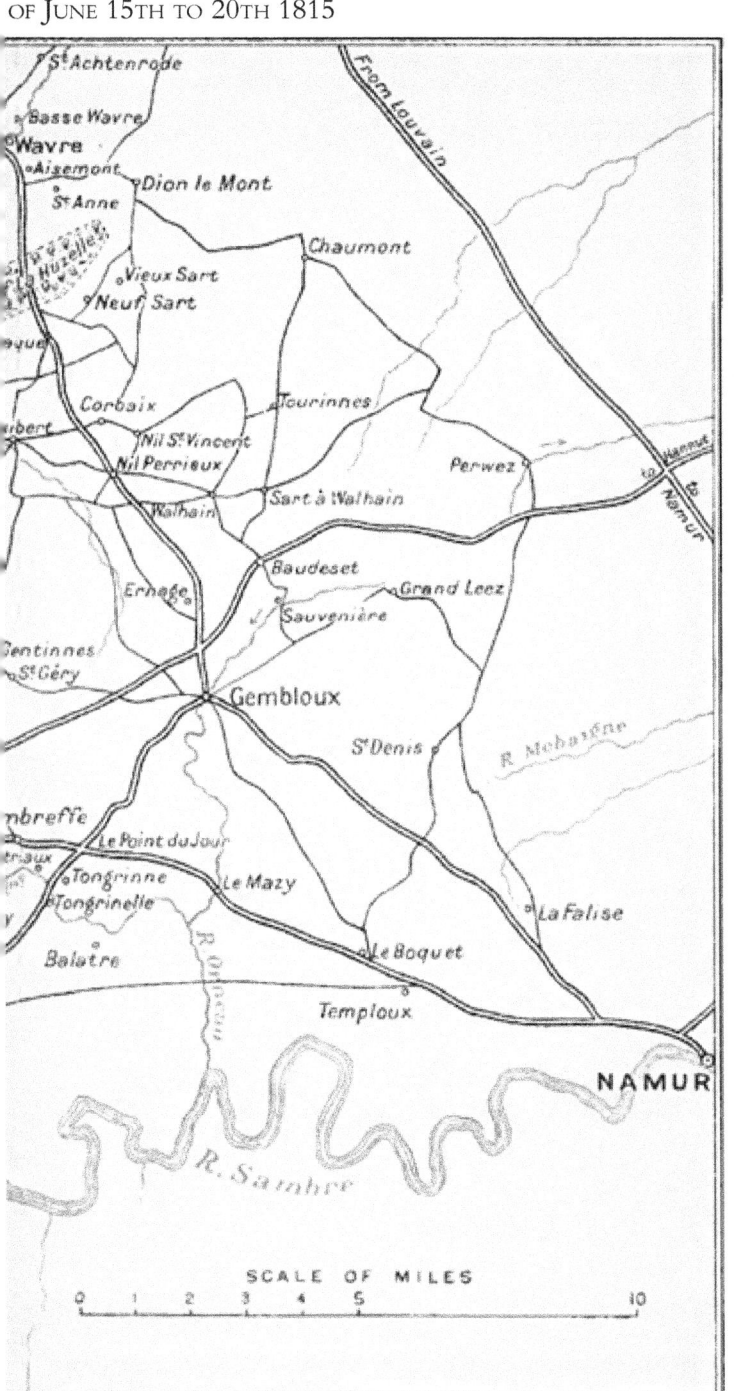

Extracts From
"The Campaign of 1815"
By William O'Connor Morris

The defeat of Ligny having forced Blücher away from Sombreffe, Wellington would be compelled to retreat from Quatre Bras. The allied chiefs, therefore, had virtually lost their natural and proper line of junction—the lateral road from Nivelles to Namur; if they did not fall back on their respective bases, they would be obliged to retire into a most intricate country, where in any case it would be difficult in the extreme to bring their divided armies together, and where Napoleon had it in his power all but certainly to prevent this movement. Their separation, therefore, might be considered assured—a capital object of their antagonist. In all human probability it would become wider, and this, were the campaign prolonged, would necessarily be of the greatest advantage to him—would multiply largely his chances of reaching his enemies when apart, and of defeating them in detail.

More than this, however, was attainable on June 17; the decisive success which Napoleon had not yet won was now, it may be affirmed, within his grasp. Blücher's army had been severely worsted; it had lost not far from 30,000 men, including stragglers and fugitives beyond recall; it was short of munitions and supplies of all kinds; its heroic chief was for the moment broken down. If, taken as a whole, it had not lost its energy, and though Bülow was at hand with his corps, it could not give battle on the 17th to an enemy in anything like powerful force. Wellington, on the other hand, after the results of Ligny, was at Quatre Bras—so to speak, 'in the air'; he could not, we have said, assemble 60,000 men on that point.

As we shall see, he had assembled 45,000 only, part of these being inferior troops; he was confronted by Ney, who, having been joined by D'Erlon, was at the head of a force nearly equal in numbers—allowing for the losses he had sustained—and to a considerable extent of superior quality; and he had Napoleon on his flank, seven or eight miles distant, with an army still at least 65,000 strong, and flushed with a splendid if a dearly-bought victory. It should be observed, too, that a very considerable part of the forces of Ney and his master had not been engaged; the corps of D'Erlon had hardly fired a shot; Lobau had not taken part in the struggle at Ligny; the Imperial Guard had not suffered much; the Light Cavalry of the Guard and three-fourths of the corps of Kellermann had literally done nothing at Quatre Bras; the mailed squadrons of Milhaud were almost intact; in short, Napoleon had nearly 60,000 fresh troops, who could be directed at once against the enemy without subjecting them to any excessive effort.

In these circumstances the Emperor had the choice of two great alternative movements at least, of which either, as affairs stood, ought now to secure him a complete triumph. Should he ascertain by daybreak, as was to be assumed, what the real position of his enemies was, he might detach an insignificant force only to observe Blücher, and hang on his retreat; and then, drawing together the great mass of his forces, he might, in conjunction with Ney, fall upon Wellington, and launch 100,000 men at least against a General who had only 45,000 in hand, and that in a position in which it was almost impossible to escape. (See Note below). This movement would probably overwhelm the Duke—certainly force him to make a disastrous retreat; yet a better and more judicious movement could be made, and would have, perhaps, even more important results. Blücher's army, though beaten, was still numerous; Bülow could reach it with 30,000 men.

> Note:—Apologists of Napoleon and of the allies have concurred in concealing, as much as possible, the enormous advantages which the Emperor could have secured on June 17. The truth, however, has come out by degrees. As regards the first alternative, above mentioned, General Shaw Kennedy (*Battle of Waterloo*) says: 'Napoleon's operations, up to the evening of the 16th, had, in their general result, been successful by Blücher's being defeated and separated from Wellington; but, to reap the fruits of his combinations and success over Blücher, it became necessary to strike against Wellington with the utmost rapidity and vigour; and it was impossible that circumstances could have been more favourable for his doing so than those which actu-

ally existed on the morning of the 17th. The Prussian army was in full retreat. Wellington's army, not yet fully collected, stood only seven or eight miles from Napoleon's, and Ney was in contact with Wellington's front. Wellington's left was completely exposed, and stood on the great *chaussée*, by which *chaussée* Napoleon had the immense advantage of being able to advance perpendicularly to the line of the Anglo-allied army, and thus to attack it to the greatest advantage before it was by any means fully in junction, and on its left flank at right angles to its line of battle; while simultaneously with Napoleon's attack on the left Ney would have assailed Wellington's front. . . . Napoleon should have led his last man and horse against the Anglo-allied army, even had the risk been great in the highest degree, which, as has been seen, it clearly was not. Had Napoleon attacked the Anglo-allied army with his whole force, and succeeded in defeating it, there could be little question of his being able to defeat afterwards the Prussian army when separated from Wellington. See also Ropes, *Campaign of Waterloo*. This alternative seemed the best to Soult, who knew better than Napoleon what British soldiers were: H. Houssaye, *Waterloo*, ii.

Napoleon was therefore bound to be on his guard against it, while he turned against his British antagonist. Following the precedents he had so often and so grandly made, he might pursue Blücher, and keep him in check with a restraining wing of considerable strength—from 30,000 to 40,000 men. This would at once prevent Blücher from drawing near his colleague, would possibly still further shatter the Prussian army, and would secure the communications of the Emperor from attack; and, having taken this precaution, Napoleon might still assail Wellington with from 70,000 to 80,000 men—that is, in immensely superior numbers—and equally gain a victory that should be decisive. (This was the second alternative; the history of war from the days of Turenne to those of Napoleon proves that it was by many degrees the best. See *Comment.*, v. It was that which Napoleon adopted, but it was adopted many hours too late; it was miserably executed by a most incompetent lieutenant. Charras 1 and 2 sums up what Napoleon could have accomplished on the 17th; it will be observed he suggests a third alternative—falling on Blücher instead of Wellington. This is also suggested by Clausewitz; but obviously, as Jomini has pointed out, it was the least judicious course.)

There was no reason that Napoleon should not give directions for either operation by four in the morning; in either case part of his forces, whether small or large, could be on the track of the Prussians by five or six, following the lines of their retreat, which the simplest diligence ought to have discovered several hours before; and the great body of his forces and those of Ney could be in front of Wellington and on his flank by eight or nine. In one event or the other the Emperor must have triumphed, and it deserves notice that nothing more was required than the insight, the energy, and the decision he had exhibited over and over again, and that in not an extraordinary degree.

Napoleon could have obtained these results; it is not difficult, after the event, to see what he might have achieved at this conjuncture. Had he been seconded as he ought to have been—above all, had he been the Napoleon of 1796 to 1809—it is probable in the extreme that he would have secured them. We proceed to consider how the immense success that was within his reach on June 17 was all but lost to him, and Fortune became adverse.

Napoleon, we have said, had returned to Fleurus, his headquarters, after Ligny; he reached that place at about eleven at night; he gave orders to Grouchy, in command of the French right, to pursue in a general way the Prussian army, with the cavalry of Excelmans and Pajol. It is said, indeed, that he indicated the probable lines of retreat—that is, northwards by the villages of Tilly and Gentinnes, the direction being taken by the corps of Zieten and Pirch, and eastwards along the roads from Sombreffe to Namur—that is, towards the communications which Thielmann had so jealously guarded.[1]

The Emperor then retired to rest, utterly exhausted, as he had been on the night of the 15th; it appears certain that he saw no one, and had no conversation on the position of affairs until between six and seven in the morning.

★★★★★★

The Emperor left Fleurus at about nine o'clock, accompanied by Grouchy, who for some time had been awaiting his orders in vain. Grouchy has remarked that his master was 'extremely fatigued.' Napoleon, unable to bear the jolting of his carriage, mounted a horse, and drove at rather a slow pace to Ligny, He was in an irritable and

---

1. Jomini (*The Campaign of Waterloo 1815*, by Antoine Henri Jomini also published by Leonaur) says that Napoleon ordered General Monthyon, an officer in the highest place on the staff of Soult, to follow the Prussians in the direction of Tilly and Gentinnes; but he gives no authority. The order, if given, was not carried into effect.

unsettled mood; he sharply told Grouchy he would give him his commands as soon as the fitting moment had come. The field of battle presented an appalling spectacle; the villages in which the conflict had raged were choked with the dead and untented wounded; Ligny was a heap of ruins, and of mutilated and charred corpses. The French army, however, was in the joyous mood of the Gaul; the sounds of the multitudinous cheers which greeted its chief were heard three or four miles off by a Prussian rearguard, covering cautiously the retreat of Pirch and Zieten. The Emperor passed his victorious troops in review, thanking officers and men and distributing rewards; he properly gave orders for the relief of the wounded, attending especially to the Prussians, ill treated by the Belgian peasants, in return for many acts of oppression; he spent some time in talking about the state of France, and the Jacobinism and folly of Parisian politics.

★★★★★★

It was now about eleven in the forenoon.[2] Napoleon gave Grouchy his long-expected orders; he still believed that Blücher was retreating towards his base, still probably unable to take the field, though Excelmans' report had turned his attention to Gembloux, a place north of the roads to Namur and Liege. There have been many discussions as to the exact terms of these orders, but their plain and general import is not doubtful. According to the version given by Grouchy, the Marshal was to pursue the Prussians, to attack them and to complete their defeat, and not to lose sight of them in any event. The Emperor added that he was about to join Ney, to attack the English army should it make a stand on the southern verge of the Forest of Soignies—a great wood between Quatre Bras and Brussels.

He closed his remarks by directing Grouchy to correspond with him by the lateral road from Nivelles to Namur, running at Quatre Bras, we have seen, into the great main-road from Charleroy to Brussels often referred to.[3] So far all the different accounts coincide, but Napoleon has subjoined an important statement: Grouchy was always

---

2. Houssaye has fixed this time, and, indeed, the time of all the operations of the 17th, as we have said, conclusively.

3. It is fair to give the *ipsissima verba* of Grouchy's version (*Observations sur la Relation de la Campagne de 1815*), cited by Charras (1) and by H. Houssaye (*1815 Waterloo*, by Henry Houssaye, also published by Leonaur): 'Mettez-vous à la poursuite des Prussiens. Complétez leur défaite en les attaquant des que vous les aurez joints, et ne les perdez jamais de vue. Je vais me réunir au Maréchal Ney pour attaquer les Anglais, s'ils tiennent de ce côté-ci de la forêt de Soignes. Vous correspondrez avec moi par la route pavée (route de Namur aux Quatre-Bras).'

to hold a position between the Prussian army and the great main-road on which the Emperor was to advance; he was thus to be in constant communication with his chief, and to be able to come into line with him. Gérard has positively said that this last order was given; that Napoleon pointedly remarked to Grouchy: 'Press the enemy hardly, and, above all, be always in contact with me by your left.'[4]

It is possible to argue about the Emperor's words; but Grouchy's force was a restraining wing; his duty, therefore, was not only to attack the Prussians, to defeat them if he could, to hold Blücher in check, but also to interpose between the allied chiefs; and this is exactly what the passage in dispute implies.[5] There is a presumption, accordingly, all but equal to proof, that Napoleon gave the order in question. Grouchy accepted it, we shall see, in this very sense, though he has dishonestly endeavoured to conceal the truth. The responsibility of a weighty charge alarmed Grouchy; nor was his anxiety without sufficient cause. He may have remembered how, years before, he had failed to seize Cork, in the absence of Hoche, this being certainly within his power, and how completely he had miscarried at Bantry; he had never had a great independent command; he was a good cavalry officer, but unfit to be a General-in-Chief. Besides, he had already quarrelled with Vandamme, a malevolent and wrong-headed man; and he was well aware that Vandamme and Gérard considered themselves, as they were, very superior to him, and chafed at being placed under the Marshal's command.

Grouchy, he tells us,[6] remonstrated with his master; pointed out that the Prussians were far off in retreat; that they had gained 'fourteen hours' upon their pursuers; that the French troops at Ligny had not expected to march that day, and that they would be unable to march for a considerable time. The Marshal added that he feared he could not hold Blücher in check; that he had not sufficient force with 33,000 men to restrain an army still 90,000 strong; that the Prussians

---

4. Thiers, *Histoire du Consulat et de l'Empire,* vi. Thiers says he had the very words from the lips of Gérard—no friend of Grouchy, but an honourable man. Napoleon's version of this order will be found in *Comment,* v.: '*Grouchy avait l'ordre positif de se tenir toujours entre la chaussée de Charleroi à Bruxelles et Blücher; afin d'être constamment en communication, et en mesure de se réunir sur l'armée.*'

5. Jomini (*The Campaign of Waterloo* 1815) has no real doubt but that Napoleon's version of his orders to Grouchy is substantially correct. '*Il est de mon devoir d'observer que l'ordre mentionné dans la relation de Ste. Hélène, était tellement conforme au système des lignes intérieurs au quel Napoléon avait dû le plus grand nombre de ses victoires, qu'en ne saurait révoquer en doute qu'il l'ait effectivement donné.*'

6. Grouchy, *Observations sur la Campagne de 1815,* quoted at length by La Tour d'Auvergne, *Waterloo.*

appeared to be falling back on Namur; and that, if this were the case, he would be at a great distance from the main army and widely divided from it, Napoleon, Grouchy has alleged, was not pleased with these remarks; asked him angrily, it has been said, 'was he to give him lessons?' and repeated, as was the fact, 'that it was Grouchy's business to ascertain the line of the enemy's retreat.'[7]

A short time after this interview, such as it was—that is, at about half-past eleven o'clock—Napoleon sent another order to Grouchy, expressed in positive and unambiguous terms.[8] Soult had lingered at Fleurus and had not yet reached Ligny; the Emperor dictated the letter to Bertrand, the most trusted, perhaps, of his surviving officers; Grouchy certainly received it before noon. This order is one of the highest importance; it was most discreditably suppressed by Grouchy, who even denied that it had an existence; it was not unearthed until 1842. It has been slurred over by the worshippers of success, by apologists for the allies, by Napoleon's detractors; to this hour it has hardly received the close attention it deserves, but it sets forth clearly the ideas of the Emperor at the time, and throws a flood of light on the subsequent conduct of Grouchy.[9]

In this remarkable paper the Emperor orders Grouchy to march on Gembloux with the mass of his forces—that is, to turn away from the roads towards Namur and Liége, supposed hitherto to be the only line of Blücher's retreat, and to occupy a place leading northwards on the roads to Brussels—that is, in a direction completely different. Napoleon then desires his lieutenant to reconnoitre the 'roads to Na-

---

7. H. Houssaye (*1815 Waterloo*) has given us good reasons for suspecting that this alleged conversation between Grouchy and Napoleon was either imaginary or has been misrepresented. Grouchy is, we repeat, not to be trusted in his statements. He hardly could have told the Emperor that the Prussians had gained 'fourteen hours' on him, when the time was not more than ten or twelve, and when Excelmans was in touch with them at Gembloux. He hardly could have said that the retreat of the Prussians was on Namur, when it was known that Gembloux was largely occupied by them. There are many other inconsistencies.

8. It is questionable whether the new order was made upon the information already given by Excelmans, or upon fresh information supplied by General Berton: H. Houssaye, *Waterloo*, 2; Charras, 1.

9. This despatch was first published in a work called *Notice Biographique sur le Maréchal Grouchy*, Paris, 1842. It will be found at length in La Tour d'Auvergne, *Waterloo*. Grouchy repeatedly denied that it existed (*Observations sur la Campagne de 1815*; cited by Houssaye, *1815 Waterloo*), and, when confronted by the fact, changed the hour of its reception from the forenoon to three o'clock, a scandalous misrepresentation: H. Houssaye, *ante*.

mur and Maastricht,' to 'pursue the enemy,' and to correspond with headquarters by the lateral road from Nivelles to Namur, joining the great main road from Charleroy to Brussels, observing again that he was going in person to Quatre Bras. The despatch nearly ends with these most significant words: 'It is important to ascertain what are the enemy's designs; he is either separating from the English, or both are seeking to unite in order to cover Brussels or Liége, and to try the chances of another battle;' and it concludes with an injunction to Grouchy to keep all his troops well in hand.

From this pregnant testimony we can fully gather what was passing in Napoleon's mind at this moment. He probably still suspects that Blücher is falling back on his base—at least, with the chief part of his forces; he therefore directs Grouchy to observe the roads to Namur and Maastricht, and to dog the enemy's movements in that direction. But evidently he is greatly struck by the reports he has just received, that the Prussians are in large numbers at Gembloux, so he commands Grouchy to repair to that place, where he would at once all but certainly come in touch with the enemy, and where, too, he would be on the way to Brussels; and he then plainly points out that it was quite possible that Wellington and Blücher would endeavour to join hands in order to defend Brussels, and to run the risk of a battle. The order accordingly proves that Napoleon, if perhaps still sceptical, was nevertheless alive to the contingency that the allies would try to unite; and it indicates distinctly that it was Grouchy's mission to keep Wellington and Blücher apart.[10]

---

10. Mr. Ropes (*Campaign of Waterloo*) is one of the very few commentators who have seen the full significance of this despatch. We quote these just and discriminating observations: ' There is in this letter no trace of that certainty as to the position of affairs so plainly exhibited in the verbal orders. The news that a Prussian corps has been seen at Gembloux has evidently made a strong impression on the Emperor. It may very possibly indicate that Blücher is not falling back to Namur. The statement is twice made in the letter that the Emperor is in doubt as to the intentions of the Prussians, and the chief task now imposed upon Grouchy is to ascertain those intentions. The precise danger to be anticipated is stated explicitly. Grouchy is warned in so many words that the Prussians may be intending to unite with the English, to try the fate of another battle for the defence of Brussels, which was exactly what they were intending to do, and what they succeeded in doing. Whether they are or are not intending to do this is the principal thing for Grouchy to find out.' Mr. Ropes (*Campaign*) is also properly severe on those commentators, for the most part English, who either ignore or give no weight to a document of supreme importance. But the object of these writers is obvious: they seek (1) to show that Napoleon never had any inkling of the designs of Blücher and Wellington, (continued next page),

★★★★★★

We pass on to the movements of Grouchy, of supreme importance for the results of the contest, but misrepresented or ill-explained for years, and even now not completely explained. The Marshal lost no time in assembling his army when he had received the despatch of his master written by Bertrand; he was one of those men who blindly depend on superior orders, but who, without initiative and clear insight, are often unable to comprehend their full import, and, catching at a shadow, drop the real substance. At about noon his 33,000 men were under arms,[11] and ready to begin the march to Gembloux, the direction their chief had been enjoined to take.

We must bear in mind what his position was at this moment. Pajol, we have seen, had come up with the enemy on the way to Namur; but he soon discovered that he was in contact with stragglers only, and that the Prussians were not, on that line, in force; he returned to Mazy and halted there for some hours, having heard from peasants that a large part of the hostile army was in retreat by St. Denis and Leuze towards Louvain, that it was moving away from its communications with Namur and Liége, was marching northwards, and drawing towards Brussels.

It would appear that Pajol did not send this report to Grouchy for a considerable time, but Grouchy, like Napoleon, had been made aware that the Prussians were around Gembloux 'in great force,' and that Excelmans was on his way to reach them, and Gembloux was the point Grouchy was himself to attain.

This intelligence ought to have made the Marshal reflect that, in all probability, the Prussian army was abandoning the direction of Namur and Liege, and was not falling back on its base at all; it certainly ought to have induced him to advance on Gembloux and to find out the enemy without the loss of an instant; and it is fair to remark that Grouchy seems at first to have had the latter object distinctly in view. He had assembled his forces with praiseworthy haste, but the march to Gembloux was made extraordinarily slow, and was retarded by a

---

to unite after Ligny and Quatre Bras; (2) to justify the essentially faulty, in point of strategy, operations of the allies on the 17th, which, indeed, gained Waterloo, but ought to have lost it; and (3) to exculpate or excuse Grouchy, and to throw on Napoleon the whole blame of the disaster of June 18. It is the duty of history to overthrow the superstructure of misrepresentation and sophistry which has been raised in consequence.

11. The time is fixed by M. H. Houssaye (*Waterloo*, 2) by absolutely conclusive evidence.

series of delays, largely to be ascribed to Grouchy himself. The corps of Gérard around Ligny was the nearest to Gembloux, and should have been the first to move; but Grouchy, afraid to annoy Vandamme, whose corps was at St. Amand, some distance to the left, placed Vandamme and his troops at the head of the columns on their march; nearly two hours were thus unnecessarily lost. In addition Gembloux might have been reached by at least two roads; but Grouchy crowded his army into one column on a single road, and this again greatly retarded his march.

The result was that Vandamme did not reach Gembloux until seven o'clock, and Gérard not until nine in the evening; and yet Gembloux is only eight miles from Ligny, and not more than ten from St. Amand. Unquestionably the storm and bad roads had impeded the march; but these obstacles had been overcome by the Prussians, who had moved at a very different rate of speed; and Napoleon had made a march of twenty miles at least, and that in the presence of an enemy in his front, even if he had the advantage of the great main-road from Charleroy to Brussels. Meanwhile Thielmann, whose corps had been reached by Excelmans, and who, we have seen, had halted at Gembloux a great deal too long, had been allowed to escape almost unobserved; and Excelmans, who on this eventful day seems to have been as overconfident and careless as most of his fellows, had advanced only to Sauvenière, a village two or three miles beyond Gembloux, and did not hang with his horsemen on the retreat of the enemy.

This was an inauspicious beginning of a pursuit which ought to have been pressed with all the more celerity because it had been undertaken very late. By the night of the 17th the whole Prussian army was being gathered together around Wavre—that is, ten or eleven miles from Waterloo—while Grouchy's army, scarcely more than a third in numbers, was at or near Gembloux—that is, at least sixteen miles from Napoleon's camp. These distances were already not of happy omen. Nevertheless, whatever has been said, there was still no reason that Grouchy should not be able successfully to perform his task, should not be able to reach and to attack the enemy—above all, should not hold Blücher fast, and keep him away from Wellington, fulfilling the true part of a restraining wing, if he had the capacity of anything like a real chief.

In the course of the night Grouchy received numerous reports, all indicating that the Prussians were in retreat northwards; had abandoned their communications with Namur and Liége; and were either making for Wavre, as the fact was, or for Perwez, in the direction of Louvain, the evidence preponderating that Wavre was the object of their march. Excelmans pushed forward some squadrons to Nil St. Vincent and Sart les Walhain, villages only seven or eight miles from Wavre, and heard that the enemy was on his way to that place; a detachment sent to Perwez gave the same intelligence. The inhabitants of Gembloux and the peasantry of the adjoining tract—in sympathy with the French, and hating the Prussians—spoke of Prussian movements on Perwez or Wavre; there was even a rumour that Blücher was trying to join Wellington—that is, was near Wavre—with the intention of reaching Waterloo.[12]

Upon this information, surely significant enough, Grouchy wrote to Napoleon at ten at night. This despatch should also be studied with care. In this communication the Marshal tells his master that he is at Gembloux and his cavalry at Sauvenière; that the enemy, '35,000 strong,' is retreating; that the Prussians were divided into two main columns, one moving on Wavre, the other on Perwez; that a third column was falling back on Namur; that a part of these forces, 'it might be inferred,' was 'on the way' to join hands with Wellington, and that another part was perhaps making ultimately for Liége. The Marshal adds that he was sending his cavalry forward, and that, according to the intelligence it should bring in, he would march either on Wavre or Perwez. The despatch ends with these most important words, showing plainly that Grouchy understood his mission: 'If the great body of the Prussians is retiring upon Wavre, I will follow them in that direction, so that they shall not be able to reach Brussels, and that I may separate them from Wellington.'[13]

The information Grouchy had already obtained should have led him to conclude that the Prussian army was, for the most part, at least, assembling at Wavre. But considering it even from his own point of view, the course he ought to adopt should have been plain to his mind. He might disregard any hostile force on its way to Perwez—that is, to Louvain—for this was in far eccentric retreat, and could neither molest Napoleon nor assist Wellington. But he was bound to follow without delay, and carefully to attack and hold in check, any

---

12. H. Houssaye, *1815 Waterloo*.
13. This despatch will be found in La Tour d'Auvergne, *Waterloo*. Grouchy shamefully garbled it afterwards, feeling the full significance, regard being had to his subsequent conduct, of the expression that he would 'separate' the Prussians from Wellington: Ropes, *The Campaign of Waterloo*.

hostile force making for Wavre; for this obviously was drawing near Wellington—nay, might be seeking to come to his aid; and this was the more necessary because the Emperor had told Grouchy that it was his intention to attack the English in front of the Forest of Soignies, distant only ten or eleven miles from Wavre.

The means of securing the Marshal's object and of enabling him to fulfil his duty were not difficult, and ought to have been apparent. He ought to advance on Wavre as quickly as possible, and so to direct his march as to have the power to strike Blücher in flank were he trying to join Wellington; and this operation was possible—nay, quite feasible. Gembloux is some fifteen miles from Wavre, and from the roads on which the Prussians would march in case they were on their way to Waterloo; it is about ten miles from the Dyle at Moustier and Ottignies, whence there were roads to Wavre, to the line of the enemy's possible movement, and to the positions now held by Napoleon.

The course for Grouchy to take was, therefore, as it were, marked out; he should make for Wavre by daybreak on June 18; but he should direct his movement to the Dyle at Moustier and Ottignies, crossing the river at these points by the bridges, which, like those on the Sambre, remained intact; it would be then within his power either to advance on Wavre, should the Prussians be remaining at that place, or to attack Blücher, to hold him in check for a space of time, sufficiently long, at least, to prevent him giving support to his colleague—and the attack, we must bear in mind, would be on Blücher's flank, and about as perilous as could be conceived—and especially to co-operate with the main French army should the Emperor be in need of his aid. Had Grouchy formed this resolution on the night of June 17, and carried it out intelligently on the following morning, he would have atoned for the faults even now to be laid to his charge; Blücher, humanly speaking, could never have joined Wellington; Waterloo could never have been a victory for the allies.

The lines taken by the Prussians in their retreat from Ligny ought to have been ascertained by the dawn of June 17. For this Soult was responsible, in the first instance; but Napoleon, too, must be held responsible—they would have been discovered had he been the Napoleon of old. Grouchy was sent to find them out, but many hours too late; and his march on Gembloux had been so retarded, and Excelmans had given proof of so little zeal and skill, that the direction taken by the enemy remained uncertain. But the evidence obtained by Grouchy on the night of the 17th pointed in the main to a retreat on

Wavre. It did not really point to a retreat on Perwez; the movement on Wavre was the one most probable, and the only one that could endanger Napoleon; Grouchy, therefore, we repeat, ought to have provided against it by adopting the measures before referred to; had he done this he would have redressed the many shortcomings and mistakes of the day; he would have stopped Blücher on his way to Waterloo; he would have averted from France a frightful disaster.

No remarkable insight or energy were required; besides, independently of the reports before him, he ought to have acted in the spirit of his orders—and these he understood—and to have so conducted his operations as in any event to interpose between the allied commanders. He ought, in a word, to have borne in mind that in war, should a doubt exist, a general should assume that his enemy would do what is best for his interests, and that the military art is one of a fine calculation of chances, and of making the most of the opportunities these may present.[14]

Unfortunately Grouchy was one of those chiefs who cling to the letter and miss the real import, and are incapable of bold and original movements. He never even thought of directing his army on Moustier and Ottignies; he did not move a division on the night of the 17th towards these points; he did not contemplate an early or rapid march on Wavre—nay, even a march on Wavre at all—though he had indicated Wavre as the place on which he would move should he learn that the enemy was there in force. On the contrary, his orders show that he was chiefly thinking of making his way towards Perwez—that is, to his right, far away from Napoleon, and not toward Wavre, where the Prussian army was; Vandamme and Excelmans were to advance to Sart les Walhain; Gérard was to follow the movement, and to send his horse to Grand Leez, ' for the enemy was falling back on Perwez'; Pajol was to march to Grand Leez from Mazy. The truth seems to be that he had taken it into his head that the Prussians were retreating on Perwez—that is, in the last event, on Louvain—and that his only duty was to follow and attack Blücher; he did not reflect that his paramount duty—and yet he was fully aware of this—was to play the part of a

---

14. This is well put by Charras (2): '*Grouchy devait tirer sa résolution des circonstances. En pareil cas, l'hésitation n'est pas permis: il faut baser ses opérations sur la supposition qui son adversaire a agit at agira pour atteindre le resultat le plus favorable à ses intérêts et conformement au caractère qu'on lui connait. Il n'y a pas d'autre règle de conduite rationnelle. L'art du général serait bien vulgaire, si on n'avait jamais à opérer que sur des ordres parfaits, sur des données certaines.*'

commander of a restraining wing, and to interpose between Blücher and Wellington.

Leaving Grouchy blindly following a fatal course, we turn to Napoleon, now before Waterloo. There was no sign in him on the night of the 17th of the sluggish lethargy clearly seen in the morning. He superintended in person the positions occupied by his troops, placed D'Erlon, Milhaud, Domon, Subervie, Lefebvre-Desnoëttes—in fact, the parts of his army at present on the spot—in a line extending from Plancenoit to Monplaisir, and sent pressing orders that Lobau, the Imperial Guard and Reille should come into line from the rear as quickly as possible. A farmhouse called Caillou was made his headquarters, but he took little rest on this memorable night. Wellington and his army were now in his front, but Napoleon feared that his adversary would not offer him battle; he believed that the Duke and Blücher, conforming to judicious strategy, would retire behind Brussels, combine their forces, and then make ready to meet him in overwhelming numbers; he would not be given again, he supposed, the opportunities given at Ligny and Quatre Bras.

His leading idea—and this almost engrossed his mind—was to bring the British commander to bay before he could decamp and join his colleague; he did not seriously think that Blücher, wherever he might be, would venture to make a flank march of the most perilous kind on the chance of being able to reach Wellington; in his heart of hearts he was convinced, with all his lieutenants, that the Prussian army was not yet in a condition to fight. Above all, had he not despatched Grouchy many hours before to pursue it, to attack it, to make it impossible that it should come to the assistance of the Duke's army, should it even have the power of giving battle?

A report from Milhaud that an enemy's column was making for Wavre—this was the detachment called in from Tilly—did not affect the Emperor's fixed belief; he refused to suppose that Blücher could march from Wavre on Waterloo; besides, this might be only a stray column endeavouring to approach Brussels, whither we had seen Blücher, he thought, might march. It appears to be probable, nevertheless, that on receiving this news Napoleon sent a message to Grouchy;[15] but if this was the case, it never reached the Marshal; and certainly Blücher and the Prussian army were not uppermost at this moment in the Emperor's mind. Napoleon left his headquarters after midnight to observe the positions of the hostile army; he contemplated, he has

---

15. H. Houssaye, *1815 Waterloo.*

informed us, a night attack should the Duke be showing signs of retreat; his orders prove this statement to be correct. But all was silence in the enemy's camps; 'the Forest of Soignies looked like a conflagration; the horizon shone with bivouac fires';[16] the only sounds were the faint rumble of guns, and the dash of the torrents of rain that had not ceased to fall. Napoleon returned to his farmhouse, hopeful, but not satisfied; his adversary was evidently making a stand; but would the state of the weather permit an attack to be made?

At about two in the morning the message arrived, sent by Grouchy at ten on the night of the 17th. This despatch, it should be borne in mind, was calculated to inspire Napoleon with complete confidence as to the possible operations of Blücher on June 18. The Prussian army was represented as not being in great force, and as divided into two, or even three, columns, falling back on Wavre, Perwez, and Namur; and the Marshal had pledged himself that were it moving on Wavre, in considerable strength, he would take care 'to separate Blücher from Wellington.' The Emperor felt that he need have no fears as to his veteran enemy; his lieutenant understood his duty, and would hold him in check; he had only to direct his whole forces against Wellington, the opinion he had already held for some time.

It is probable, however, that, before he had heard from Gembloux, he had formed a design of attracting part of the forces of Grouchy, and in certain circumstances the principal part, to the scene of the great battle obviously now at hand, and that he adhered to the design after Grouchy's message. We have reached one of the most perplexing episodes of the campaign, which has not received sufficient attention, and on which just enough light has been thrown to make the darkness, so to speak, more visible. Napoleon has positively asserted that he sent two messages on the night of the 17th, directing Grouchy to send a detachment of 7,000 men and sixteen guns to St. Lambert, a little village near the Lasne, about four miles from the French lines, and to fall at an early hour on the left flank of Wellington; the Marshal was to support the movement, with the mass of his army, when he had ascertained the whereabouts of Blücher.[17] This statement has been summarily rejected by most critics, but their arguments seem to

---

16. H. Houssaye, *1815 Waterloo*.
17. *Comment.* v. An attentive student of war will observe how these alleged orders conformed to Napoleon's statement that when he detached Grouchy, on the morning of the 17th, he directed the Marshal to keep between Blücher and the great main-road from Charleroy to Brussels.

us of no great weight; the reasons to the contrary are so cogent and so increasing in force. There is literally nothing in the circumstance that no such orders can be found on the records of the Chief of the French Staff; the same remark applies to the all-important order written by Bertrand in the absence of Soult.

Nor is there much in the circumstance that the orders in question seem to be inconsistent with a well-known despatch of Soult, written in the forenoon of June 18, to which we shall advert afterwards. Napoleon may not have consulted Soult, with whom he was by no means satisfied; he may have thought it advisable to keep his counsel to himself. There are solid grounds, on the other hand, for accepting the Emperor's distinct assertion. The movement on St. Lambert was exactly in Napoleon's manner; it was the counterpart of the movement on Marbais, which Ney was ordered to make on the 16th; it was in accord with the plan of attack at Waterloo. Again there is clear evidence from independent sources that Napoleon expected Grouchy to be in line with him at an early hour on June 18; this most pregnant fact has only been lately disclosed, but it is of extreme significance, and we shall recur to it.

Finally, it is not to be assumed that, in a matter of this kind, the Emperor deliberately wrote a downright falsehood; this is very different from the inaccurate and partial statements to be found in his narratives of the campaign, and recent investigation, it should be added, has tended to confirm, in the main, these writings. On the whole, we incline to think these orders were given; this would account for much that is now obscure; but unquestionably they never reached Grouchy; he would have been too eager, if they had, to comply with them. The bearers of the despatches may have been killed or made prisoners; and unhappily there were traitors and deserters in the French army.[18]

★★★★★★

The plan of the allied commanders, therefore, was this: Wellington, with an army of about 70,000 men, of whom scarcely 40,000 were really good troops, was to resist the attack of Napoleon in immensely superior force, regard being had to the quality of his army. Blücher was to march from Wavre to the aid of his colleague, each being divided from the other by ten or eleven miles of a very impracticable and intricate country. It should be remarked, too, and this is important, that Wellington and Blücher both thought that all Napoleon's army was before Waterloo, with the single exception of the corps of Vandamme;

---

18 See Thiers, *Histoire du Consulat et de l'Empire*, vi.

they had no conception that Grouchy was approaching Wavre with an army fully 33,000 strong.[19]

These dispositions secured a great and decisive triumph; they have been extolled by the courtiers of fortune; but they cannot mislead an impartial student of war; they were essentially ill-designed, and hazardous in the extreme. They implied, from the allied point of view, that Wellington was to withstand Napoleon at the head of nearly 100,000 men, with an army really not half as strong, for a space of certainly five or six hours, in all probability of many more. Was this combination likely to succeed? was it not rather big with the promise of a French victory?[20] They implied, too, in the actual situation of affairs, that Blücher would surely be able to reach Waterloo, though Grouchy, with a powerful restraining wing, was gathering on his flank. The history of many a campaign has shown that the chances were that this movement would be arrested, and that Wellington would be left without support from his colleague. This strategy, therefore, was in principle bad; it ought to have proved in the highest degree disastrous; but it was the natural result of the faulty arrangement, which directed the Prussian army to Wavre, divided from Waterloo by practically a great interval of space, and which prompted the resolve to march from Wavre on Wellington.

★★★★★★

Napoleon and Wellington had now met, for the first time; each drew his lot from the urn with a steady hand; each was confident as to the issue of the impending struggle. Yet there was much in the situation as it existed, and as it appeared to both, that might have caused apprehension as to coming events. For aught the Emperor knew, his adversary had his whole army assembled; if so, it would largely exceed the French army in numbers. He had had no experience of the qualities of British troops; but Salamanca, Vittoria, and many other fields were ominous signs of what they could do in battle; he had a General before him who had never known defeat; had baffled and beaten his best lieutenants; had overthrown his gigantic power in Spain. And Blücher, wherever he was, could not be far off; and Blücher had, over and over again, confounded his calculations by his heroic energy.

---

19. *Wellington Despatches*, xii. 478 *et seq.*
20. Napoleon (*Comment.* v.) has put this view of the case forward with admirable clearness and force. Clausewitz, cited by Mr. Ropes (The Waterloo Campaign), has in vain attempted a reply. Mr. Ropes easily disposes of his very disingenuous and untrue remarks in a few sentences.

Could Napoleon rely on Grouchy with complete trust? might not the old warrior, threefold Grouchy in strength, appear at Waterloo and turn decisively the scales of fortune? And Napoleon must have felt that this was his last chance; were he to fail in this hazard, Europe in arms—nay, an exasperated France—would make him their victim. Nevertheless these thoughts had no fears for that soaring spirit, exulting within its proper sphere—war; the sun about to rise would see the ruin of the British army; and were the British army out of the way, 'of what use would be the other armies about to cross the Rhine, the Alps, and the Pyrenees?'[21]

******

The junction of Blücher and Wellington would in any event be difficult in the extreme, and could only take place late; even now, had Grouchy been a capable chief—nay, had Gérard been at the head of his army—that junction could have been made impossible. And what Napoleon were to fall on Wellington at nine in the morning, as would have happened but for the state of the weather, and perhaps a grave mistake; and what if Grouchy should appear at St. Lambert in obedience to orders he might have received? Under all these conditions the probabilities were that Wellington would be defeated, and Blücher would fail.[22] Napoleon, therefore, was not 'outgeneralled'; his efforts against the British commander, especially if they were made at an early hour, would, it is likely, be attended with success. But we venture to think—and we hope we set prejudice aside—that in no event could Napoleon's success on June 18 have been complete and decisive.

He would have overwhelmed Blücher on the 16th at Ligny had Ney and D'Erlon been equal to their tasks; in that case the campaign might have closed in Belgium. He had it in his power to inflict a crushing defeat on the allies upon the following day, but owing, we believe, to a kind of suspension of his great faculties by disease, he missed the occasion as he had never missed it before; Achilles had been in a state of lethargy in his tent. If still favourable, the chances for the battle of the 18th were much less favourable than they had previously been; and many chances were becoming adverse. We cannot accept his statement, true as to June 16 and 17, that 'but for the faults of

---

21. *Comment.* v.: '*Si l'armée anglo-hollandaise eût été détruite à Waterloo, à quoi eût servi aux alliés ce grand nombre d'armées qui se disposient à franchir le Rhin, las Alps, et les Pyrénées?*' No prouder testimony could be given to the value of a British army, and to the power of England.
22. See Charras, 2, and Lord Wolseley, *Decline and Fall of Napoleon.*

his lieutenant he would have made an end of his foes at Waterloo.'[23]

★★★★★★

Napoleon estimated the Duke's army at its full normal strength,[24] 90,000 men, for he was not aware that a large body of troops had been left round Hal; he was undertaking an operation which, he has told us himself, should be avoided if possible, and must be hazardous, attacking a great master of defence in a position chosen by himself; yet he felt convinced that, with a force he calculated as 69,000 Frenchmen, he could certainly defeat—nay, destroy—a force largely superior, he thought, in number. 'The chances,' he said, 'are nine to one in our favour'; in this we see his too sanguine and sometimes presumptuous temper.

He gave little attention to the remarks or the warnings of the companions in arms seated at his board, many of these in a mood wholly different from his own. His brother Jerôme informed him that he had heard a report at Genappe that Blücher was about to march from Wavre to join Wellington. Napoleon rejected the idea as almost extravagant; should the enemies unite, it would be behind Brussels; in any case Grouchy would dispose of Blücher. Ney declared that Wellington was about to retreat, and that his columns were making for the Forest of Soignies; the Emperor replied, and in part truly: 'It is now too late; Wellington would expose himself to certain destruction; he has thrown the dice; they have turned up for us.' Napoleon even seems not to have taken much heed of the advice of lieutenants well acquainted, with the British army, and taught by bitter experience in Portugal and Spain. Reille told him that British troops in position were formidable in the very highest degree, and that he ought to try to manoeuvre them out of the ground they held. D'Erlon, it is believed, said much the same; but neither seem to have deeply impressed their master.

Of all Napoleon's subordinates, Soult was the least hopeful; even now his mind was not without forebodings. The Chief of the Staff knew, as the Emperor did not, what the qualities of a British army were; he had wished, we have seen, that Grouchy's restraining wing should be composed of a smaller force, so that the force to attack Wellington should be more powerful. 'There are men on that hill,' he observed, 'will die where they stand sooner than retreat.' Napoleon's angry retort, it is said, was: 'You think Wellington a great General be-

---

23. Napoleon Correspondence, xxxii. 275: *'Je les écrasais encore à Waterloo, si ma droite ne m'eût pas manqué.'*
24. Allowing for the losses at Quatre Bras and in the retreat.

cause he beat you; I tell you he is a bad General, and the English are bad troops; we will make a mouthful of them.'[25] Alas for genius when foredoomed by Providence! it was with Napoleon before Waterloo as it was before Moscow.

★★★★★★

It has been surmised that in coming to this resolve Napoleon had it in contemplation to gain time for Grouchy, as he expected, to reach the field in compliance with orders probably sent;[26] it has been surmised, too, that he had an intention of displaying leisurely his army in complete array before the Dutch-Belgian troops of Wellington, and so to impress them with a sense of its power; and, of course, delay made his preparations more mature, and secured time for his soldiers to rest, and to make more ready for battle. His paramount object, however, it is all but certain, was to obtain two or three hours to make the ground easier for his movements in attack. Opinions from then to now have differed as to whether this was a supremely important—nay, an attainable—object; [27] all that can be affirmed positively is that on June 18 the sun in its courses fought against Napoleon. Had the battlefield been in its ordinary state, he would have fallen on his enemies much sooner than he did; and in that event, despite Blücher's energy, and the remissness and shortcomings of Grouchy, Waterloo, humanly speaking, would have been a victory for France.

★★★★★★

We turn to Grouchy, the evil genius of France and of Napoleon,

---

25. These and other interesting details, many collected for the first time, will be found in H. Houssaye, *1815 Waterloo*.

26. Writers differing so widely as Thiers and Siborne agree in thinking that Napoleon was waiting for Grouchy to come up, but there is no trace of this in Napoleon's writings.

27. Jomini (*The Campaign of Waterloo 1815*) says: '*Quatre heures n'auraient pas suffi pour sécher un terrain comme celui la. . . . Dans la situation des affaires, ce rétard de quatre heures fut une faute.*' Charras (ii. 76, 77) is of the same opinion, and severely condemns Napoleon for the delay. On the other hand, M. Houssaye (*Waterloo*) cites authorities of weight in a contrary sense. From the point of view held by Napoleon, that Blücher would not venture to march from Wavre on Waterloo, or that if he made the attempt Grouchy would stop him, or that Grouchy would appear on the field himself, it was evidently important to let the ground become consolidated, in order to facilitate the movements of guns and horsemen. Drouot, eminently a conscientious man, was inconsolable at having given advice which proved so unfortunate in the event. See a most interesting conversation set forth in Thiers, *Histoire du Consulat et de l'Empire*, vi. The remarks of Drouot, that but for the delay a decisive victory would have been assured, are exaggerated, but contain a great deal of truth.

on the great day of Waterloo. The Marshal, we have seen, had followed the Prussians with extreme slowness on June 17; had only reached Gembloux in the evening, part of his cavalry being beyond at Sauvenière; and was thus fully fourteen miles from Blücher. This delay was certainly to be deplored; but had Grouchy fulfilled his mission, and done what his master had a right to expect, subsequent events proved that there was as yet no danger. At ten at night, we have said, he had informed the Emperor that the Prussians were in retreat not in great force either towards Wavre or towards Perwez—that is, Louvain. He had promised that, were they for the most part falling back on Wavre, he would pursue them in that direction, in order to keep Blücher apart from Wellington.

The intelligence he had already received ought, we have pointed out, to have induced him to move at daybreak on the 18th to Moustier and Ottignies, and to get over the Dyle at these places; for a march towards Perwez would be a false movement, but a march on Moustier and Ottignies would be in the true direction. It would bring him to Wavre should Blücher be halting there, would enable him to stop Blücher if on the way to Waterloo, and would draw him within easy reach of the main French army, should the Emperor be in need of his support.

Grouchy, however, had formed no such resolve, and had lingered at Gembloux; but, as the night advanced, reports came in to him which ought irrevocably to have fixed his purpose had he had a ray of the inspiration of a true soldier. He learned that the enemy was assembled around Wavre, and that without the possibility of a doubt; and at three in the morning of the 18th he wrote to the Emperor that Blücher was falling back towards Brussels in order to effect his junction with Wellington; that he was in retreat by Corbaix and Chaumont—the first a village on a line with Moustier and Ottignies, the second a village between Wavre and Perwez, and both being on the roads to Wavre—so that the Marshal's army would march at once, by Sart les Walhain, on Corbaix and Wavre.[28]

The information that the Prussians were at Wavre ought now, we repeat, to have caused Grouchy to make for Moustier and Ottignies without the delay of a moment, for the reasons we have before re-

---

28. The genuineness of this despatch has been questioned, but it seems to us to have been certainly genuine. Soult clearly refers to it in a despatch we shall notice afterwards. M. H. Houssaye contends that Grouchy wrote, not at 3 a.m., but at 6 a.m. (*1815 Waterloo*), but the text seems to be 3 a.m. Soult refers to it as written at 2 a.m. The despatch is in La Tour d'Auvergne, *Waterloo*.

ferred to; but the Marshal remained blind to his true mission, and turned aside from the path of success and safety, in an evil hour for his country and himself. He thought only of reaching his enemy, not of standing between him and his allies. The false news that Blücher had fallen back in part, by Chaumont, made Grouchy still cast his eyes towards Perwez. Instead of directing his army towards Moustier and Ottignies at break of day, he directed it towards Wavre by a rather shorter road—that is, by Sart les Walhain and the adjoining country. This was an enormous, if not a fatal, mistake. In addition, his orders were that the march was to be at a late hour; Vandamme was not to leave his camps until six in the morning, Gérard not until eight o'clock. Pajol, supported, we have said, by the division of Teste, was to march early, but by the eccentric road of Grand Leez.[29]

★★★★★★

Grouchy did not leave Gembloux even at the time, late as this was, he had originally designed. Vandamme and Gérard were not on the march until between eight and nine in the morning; as on the 17th, the troops followed each other in one huge column. The movement towards Wavre was made at the rate of little more than a mile and a half an hour. Even worse, Grouchy sent no reconnoitring-parties towards Moustier and Ottignies to bring him news of the position of the imperial army; had he taken this obvious and simple precaution, the consequences, we shall see, might have been momentous.[30]

Marbot, the author of the well-known and delightful *Memoirs*, was one of the Emperor's trusted officers; he had been made a General of Brigade after the skirmish at Genappe; he was in command on June 18 of a regiment of Jacquinot's cavalry on the extreme French right. At about eleven o'clock he received a message from Napoleon, sent through La Bédoyère, and ordering him to detach reconnoitring-parties to the bridges of Moustier and Ottignies, upon the Dyle. 'Grouchy was certainly marching towards the main army from that direction.' Marbot did what he was told to do, but found no French troops at Moustier and Ottignies; he reported the fact to the Emperor without loss of time; he was then ordered to make search for Grouchy again. 'The Marshal must be coming by the bridges of Limale and Limelette,' lower down the Dyle, and three or four miles from Wavre.[31]

---

29. These orders will all be found in La Tour d'Auvergne, *Waterloo*.
30. Mr. Ropes' narrative in treating this part of Grouchy's conduct, or, rather, misconduct, is specially good (*The Campaign of Waterloo*).
31. Marbot, *Memoirs*, iii.

This most important evidence proves that Napoleon believed that his lieutenant was approaching his camp; it is significant, in the very highest degree, that Marbot's official report on the subject was discreditably suppressed by the Bourbon Government, eager to throw the blame for Waterloo on its great fallen enemy.[32] Marbot's statement, however, unequivocal as it is, is not the only proof which distinctly points to the conclusion we have just referred to. A Polish officer, of the name of Zenowicz, made a deposition, soon after the battle, that the Emperor at about ten in the morning took him aside, and, walking up a low eminence, said, indicating the horizon to his right: 'I am awaiting Grouchy, I am awaiting him with impatience; go and join him, and do not quit his side until he debouches upon the line of my battle.'[33] It is also significant in the extreme that Zenowicz was the bearer of the despatch from Soult to Grouchy, on which we shall briefly comment at once.

This remarkable and, be it observed, independent evidence shows, as the fact was, that Napoleon had as yet no notion that Blücher was drawing near him at this conjuncture. But it shows also, what is more important, that the Emperor was convinced that Grouchy was approaching the imperial army from the Dyle; and it corroborates, with almost conclusive force, Napoleon's statement, that on the night of the 17th he twice ordered Grouchy to come to his support, with a detachment, or with the mass of his forces.

The proof could hardly admit of question, were it not confronted with the despatch written by Soult to Grouchy, to which we have just above referred. This despatch was written by Soult at ten in the morning of the 18th; it apparently is at odds with the statements of Marbot and Zenowicz; assuredly it requires to be closely studied. It was a reply to Grouchy's letter of ten on the night of the 17th, in which Grouchy, it is to be borne in mind, let his master know, among many other things, that he had not as yet made up his mind whether he would follow the Prussians by marching on Wavre or Perwez. Soult, doubtless with this letter before his eyes, informed Grouchy that the Emperor had received this report from Gembloux, but informed him further, that whereas he had referred only to two Prussian columns,

---

32. This report should, if possible, be discovered. The present writer received some time ago a courteous intimation from an authoritative source that it was not forthcoming.
33. H. Houssaye (*1815 Waterloo*), and especially Thiers (*Histoire du Consulat et de l'Empire*, vi.), who has transcribed the very words of Zenowicz.

marching by Sauvenière and Sart les Walhain—that is, in the direction of Wavre and Perwez—intelligence had been received—and this we know was the case—that a third column was moving on Wavre by Géry and Gentinnes—that is, on a line between Gembloux and the main French army. Soult then tells Grouchy that Napoleon was about to attack the English army at Waterloo, near the Forest of Soignies, and proceeds to direct Grouchy to march on Wavre—he was to reach that place as quickly as possible—and to drive away any part of the Prussian army which might be coming in that direction. The despatch next emphatically desires the Marshal 'to come near us, to connect his operations with our own, and to be in close communication with us.' This last phrase is repeated twice.[34]

Napoleon probably never saw this despatch; but, as a matter of course, he is responsible for it. It is idle, too, to contend that it does not contain an order to Grouchy to advance on Wavre, or that it is consistent, in its seeming purport, with the allegations made by Zenowicz and Marbot. But in this, as in all instances of the kind, we should endeavour to reconcile the evidence as a whole, and, gathering it together, to arrive at the real truth. This is not impossible, even not difficult, if we carefully examine and peruse the despatch, though assuredly this is most obscure—nay, misleading. Soult urges Grouchy to march on Wavre, because Grouchy was doubting whether his movement ought not to be on Perwez rather than Wavre; and Wavre, as contra-distinguished from Perwez, indisputably was the right direction to take. But Soult's despatch does not end at this point; it warns Grouchy that an enemy's column is moving on Wavre by Géry and Gentinnes—that is, between the restraining wing and the main army; it intimates that he is to attack or to intercept this; and it orders the Marshal, with marked stress of language, to come into communication with the Emperor, about to fight a decisive battle in front of Waterloo.

Now, how, in addition to a march on Wavre, was Grouchy to accomplish the two last objects, in themselves infinitely the most important, and plainly, according to the despatch, held to be the most important? The one and the only means was to take the course which he ought to have taken of his own purpose—that is, to cross the Dyle at Moustier and Ottignies, or even lower down at Limale and Limelette, and to reach Wavre by this line of march, for by this operation he would at once get to Wavre, would fall on any hostile force near

---

34. This despatch has been noticed by all historians and commentators. It is set forth at length in Prince La Tour d'Auvergne's *Waterloo*.

or around that place, and would be coming into closer relations with the imperial army. The despatch, therefore, if intelligently read, falls in with what Marbot and Zenowicz relate—and Zenowicz, we must not forget, was the bearer; it is in accord with Napoleon's belief, and probably direct orders; by implication, though not expressly, it orders Grouchy to cross the Dyle in his advance on Wavre, and on his way to draw near Napoleon, striking at the same time any enemy found in his path.[35]

The despatch, however, is ill-worded, vague, and perplexing. It ought to have stated in precise language that Grouchy should pass the Dyle before he moved on Wavre, and should send reconnoitring parties, at least, at once towards Waterloo. But Soult in this, as in other instances, proved himself to be a sorry Chief of a Staff. For the rest, writers whose object it is to charge Napoleon with an immense disaster, and to exonerate Grouchy from all blame, have found in this despatch and in another from Soult, to which we shall ere long refer, a kind of godsend in behalf of their views; but their arguments, we shall see, are mere sophistry.

★★★★★★

The cavalry scouts of Marbot, already despatched for some time towards Moustier and Ottignies, had taken an inferior Prussian officer prisoner; he carried a letter from Bülow to Wellington announcing the arrival of Bülow's corps at St. Lambert. He was brought before Napoleon, and freely answered his questions. The troops in the distance were the advanced guard of Bülow; the rest of his corps was on the march to join him. The three other corps of the Prussian army had been in bivouac around Wavre the night before, and had not had a glimpse of an enemy. The force under Grouchy, it was supposed, was on its way to Plancenoit, to come into line with the main enemy.[36]

These tidings were obviously extremely grave, but they did not greatly disconcert Napoleon. His army before Waterloo, he believed, was not yet in danger. He had received, but at a very late hour, the despatch written by Grouchy at three in the morning, and this, though less reassuring than the despatch of five hours before, was nevertheless still calculated to inspire confidence. In this letter the Marshal had

---

35. For this or nearly this view of the real meaning of Soult's despatch, see Gérard, *Dernières Observations*; Ropes, *The Campaign of Waterloo* v.; Thiers, *Histoire du Consulat et de l'Empire*, vi.; and Prince La Tour d'Auvergne, *Waterloo*.
36. *Comment.*, v. Napoleon's account is much the best, and there is no reason to question its accuracy.

informed his master that Blücher was in retreat on Brussels, in the expectation of joining Wellington; that he was falling back by Corbaix and Chaumont; and that Grouchy was on the point of moving on Sart les Walhain, whence he would proceed to Corbaix and Wavre. This indicated that Grouchy was on the track of the enemy; that whether he should march on Wavre by Moustier and Ottignies—indisputably, we have seen, his proper course—or whether he should march by Sart les Walhain and Corbaix—that is, beyond the eastern bank of the Dyle—he could not fail to hear of and to reach Blücher—Corbaix is only about six miles from Wavre—and if Blücher should be at Wavre, or making an attempt to move on Waterloo, the commander of the restraining wing, whose letters prove he understood his task, would be able to prevent Blücher from joining his ally. .The main French army, therefore, if menaced was not imperilled. Besides, the whole corps of Bülow was still distant; its advanced guard only was at St. Lambert; the remaining Prussian corps were probably far off. The battle might be won, and Wellington beaten, before Blücher could reach the field in force, should he even venture to make a most hazardous march.

Napoleon at this moment was most impressed by the fact that Grouchy's advance from Gembloux must be very slow, or otherwise he must have heard long before from the Marshal; and he was apprehensive that the detachment of 7,000 men, which he had most probably directed Grouchy to make, might be caught and destroyed by Bülow as it was approaching Waterloo. To ward off the danger as far as possible, he now ordered Lobau to follow Subervie and Domon; to choose a strong position towards St. Lambert; and to fall on the Prussians when he should hear Grouchy's guns. Bülow would then be placed between two fires; his corps, about 29,000 strong—a detachment, we have seen, had been left at Mont St. Guibert—would be in grave straits should it be assailed in front and rear by the 17,000 or 18,000 men of Lobau and by part of the troops of Grouchy. The Emperor therefore remained confident that Grouchy was at hand with a detachment of the mass of his forces, and probably by the way of

---

37. Napoleon's narrative of these incidents (*Comment.* v.) has not been sufficiently studied. It bears all the marks of truth, and proves (1) that Napoleon expected Grouchy to reach the field with the detachment at least of 7,000 men, which he had most probably ordered him to make; (2) that he did not think the main French army in danger through the apparition of Bülow; (3) that Lobau was sent towards St. Lambert, not merely to keep Bülow back, but to co-operate with Grouchy in attacking Bülow; (4) that the Emperor thought, and rightly thought, that he had little or nothing to fear from the mass of the Prussian army.

Moustier and Ottignies. If this were the case, Lobau and Grouchy would destroy Bülow, and Waterloo would be a more complete triumph for France.[37]

A short time before Bülow's troops were seen, Soult had written another despatch to Grouchy. This bears the date of one o'clock on June 18. Unquestionably it was a reply to Grouchy's message sent at three in the morning of the same day, but it alludes to Grouchy as having written an hour before.[38] This letter is as vaguely and badly worded as the previous letter of ten in the morning, but, if rightly interpreted, it bears nearly the same meaning. Soult informs Grouchy that his master generally approves of the "advance on Sart les Walhain, and thence on Corbaix and Wavre. 'This conforms to the dispositions made by His Majesty.' But while Soult sanctions the march on Wavre, he repeats the injunction to Grouchy he had made before: 'The Marshal was to manoeuvre in our direction, to come into close contact with us'; and he positively orders Grouchy to march on Waterloo, where the battle was being waged, and to 'come into line without delay with our right.'

This, again, indicates a march on Wavre, no doubt by Corbaix; but this village is on a line with Moustier and Ottignies. The despatch summons Grouchy to the field of Waterloo, and the way to accomplish this was to approach Wavre indeed, but by Moustier and Ottignies and the western bank of the Dyle. Soult then added a postscript, probably under Napoleon's eye; Grouchy was apprised that Bülow was threatening the right flank of the main army; he was emphatically commanded to 'approach and join us,' and to crush Bülow, 'who would be caught in a fatal position.' This is a strong corroboration of proof, already nearly conclusive, that the Emperor had directed Grouchy on the night of the 17th to draw near him with a detachment or the mass of his army, and that he believed Grouchy to be at a short distance, and able with Lobau to deal Bülow a mortal stroke.[39]

★★★★★★

We pass on to the operations of Grouchy, destined fatally to de-

---

38 This letter will be found in La Tour d'Auvergne, *Waterloo*. It was written in pencil, and almost illegible, like much of Soult's work. The date 2 a.m., instead of 3 a.m., is palpably a mistake.

39. If any candid inquirer will put together the positive statements of Napoleon, as regards the detachment from Grouchy, the evidence of Marbot and Zenowicz, the two letters of Soult on the 18th at 10 a.m. and 1 p.m., and this postscript, the inference to be drawn seems to us almost irresistible. The evidence, it will be observed, is independent and cumulative.

ceive his master, while on his way from Gembloux to Sart les Walhain. His march, we have seen, had been very late and very slow, faults for which he must bear the whole blame. And he had not reconnoitred in the direction of Moustier and Ottignies—that is, of the imperial army—unpardonable remissness attended with disastrous results: for had he taken this obvious step he would have ascertained how affairs stood, and soon after noon would have been in communication with Marbot's horsemen, despatched by the Emperor to bring him to the field of Waterloo.

A little before eleven o'clock the Marshal had reached Walhain, a village about a mile west of Sart les Walhain, and therefore a mile nearer Napoleon's lines. He wrote another despatch at this place to his master, which gives proof of great want of intelligence, and shows how little he had done to ascertain the facts.[40]

In this letter Grouchy informs the Emperor that Blücher was still in retreat on Brussels, but that a considerable part of the Prussian army was being assembled in the plains of the Chyse, a stream flowing towards Louvain from the north-east of Wavre. The mass of the army was probably taking this direction, perhaps in order to join Wellington at or near Brussels. The restraining wing and its chief would on the present evening be round Wavre, and so would interpose between Blücher and Wellington, the last presumed to be falling back upon Brussels.[41] It is unnecessary to point out how false this information was. So far from being in retreat on Brussels, still less from diverging into the plains of the Chyse and towards Louvain, Blücher was on the march from Wavre to Waterloo—that is, against Napoleon, not away from him.

So far from Wellington being on his way to Brussels, he was awaiting his antagonist's attack at Mont St. Jean. And from this, of course, it follows that Grouchy's purpose to advance on Wavre by the evening of the 18th, in order to be in a position between the two hostile armies, was utterly vain, being in contradiction to the facts, and was leading him most disastrously astray. It had also this further evil effect: it induced Grouchy to imagine that there was no need that he should turn his attention towards the main French army, or that he should accelerate his tardy march on Wavre. On this very evening he would

---

40. Mr. Ropes (*The Campaign of Waterloo*) is the first historian who has proved that it was not at Sart les Walhain, but Walhain, that Grouchy halted. M. H. Houssaye (1815 *Waterloo*) has added a good deal to the evidence on the subject.

41. This despatch will be found in La Tour d'Auvergne, *Waterloo*.

stand between Blücher and Wellington.[42] He was not called upon to move with increased celerity.

At this time—that is, not long after eleven o'clock—the positions held by Grouchy's army were these: The cavalry of Excelmans had pushed forward, and had reached La Baraque and the Bois d'Huzelles, points between three and four miles from Wavre; the heads of Vandamme's columns had passed Nil St. Vincent, a village some seven miles from Wavre and near Corbaix; the corps of Gérard was around Walhain and Sart les Walhain; the horsemen of Pajol and the infantry of Teste were on the march from Grand Leez to Tourinnes, and were perhaps two or three miles from Nil St. Vincent. It should be observed, too—and this is very important—the movements of Grouchy had completely escaped the notice of the Prussian detachment at Mont St. Guibert, commanded by an officer of the name of Ledebur; in fact, Excelmans and Vandamme were at this moment almost between Ledebur and the Prussian corps at Wavre.

This was the situation when Grouchy, with Gérard and other officers, who had met at Walhain—the dwelling has at last been ascertained—heard a rumbling sound towards the west at a distance. This rapidly swelled into a continuous roar. It was the thunder of the cannon of Waterloo, loud. Grouchy exclaimed, as that of Wagram. Gérard, a soldier of real insight and resource, urged his chief at once to march towards the scene of the battle, in which the Emperor was evidently engaged. Gérard's reasoning did not admit of an answer. By moving in the direction of Wellington, the restraining wing would exactly perform its task. Grouchy would stop Blücher were he halting at Wavre, or would intercept him were he on his way to Waterloo, or would come into line with the imperial army, should the hostile commanders have joined hands.

This was palpably the true—nay, the obvious—course. Nor could Grouchy conceal from himself that Blücher had gained nearly a march on him, and that Blücher's movements were not distinctly and completely known. The means, too, to make the proposed movement were easy and at hand. The cavalry in advance should seize the bridges of Moustier and Ottignies, and cross the Dyle, a march from La Baraque of about three miles; the corps of Vandamme and Gérard should fol-

---

42. It deserves notice how in this, as in other despatches, Grouchy shows that he understood the real purport of the letter he received from Napoleon through Bertrand. This he discreditably suppressed. The fact speaks for itself, and should silence his apologists.

low as quickly as possible; the horsemen of Pajol and the division of Teste should push on towards Wavre, in order to mask the operations to the left, and to make demonstrations against the enemy. Within two or three hours the position of affairs would be made plain; within five or six Grouchy would have been within reach of the Prussian or of the main French army.

The attempts made by Grouchy to answer Gérard show how disastrous it may be in war, as in other spheres of the conduct of man, to stick at the letter and to miss the essential spirit. The Marshal said that his orders were to follow the Prussians, and that this object could be best attained by marching on Wavre by the line he was taking; that the Emperor had told him that he would attack Wellington should that General make a stand before the Forest of Soignies, but that he, that is. Grouchy—and this we believe to be true—had received no command to draw near the main army; and that even were he to advance towards Waterloo, the distance was so great he could not be on the field in time.

The unfortunate chief could not, or would not, understand that Wavre could be reached by the western bank of the Dyle and by the bridges of Moustier and Ottignies almost as quickly as by any other way, if it was necessary to proceed to Wavre at all; that his paramount duty—and this he knew—was to interpose between Blücher and Wellington; that he could not possibly accomplish this should Blücher endeavour to march from Wavre on Waterloo, unless he should cross the Dyle by Moustier and Ottignies, or conceivably by Limale and Limelette; that were he to move towards the Emperor without delay, he would effectually make his presence felt hours before he should even approach Waterloo; and that in any event, in his perplexing position—due to his own remissness, inactivity, and mistakes—his only course was to press forward towards the sound of the cannon.

Grouchy, however, it is believed, would have yielded, had not Gérard's language been peremptory and his bearing stiff. The jealousy of each other, so characteristic of the warriors of France from the day of Roncesvalles to the day of Spicheren may have closed his ears to the counsel of manifest wisdom.[43] The Marshal insisted on making for Wavre along the eastern bank of the Dyle—that is, keeping completely away from Waterloo. He angrily rejected the prayer of Gérard to allow him to march with his single corps towards Napoleon. Disregarding the advice of almost all his officers—a General of Artillery

---

43. See La Tour d'Auvergne, *Waterloo*.

was the only exception, and he did not urge his objections long—and despite the angry murmurs of his own soldiery, more intelligent than their purblind leader, Grouchy directed his army to march on Wavre by the roads he had marked out for himself in the morning. Had he listened to his colleague and taken the true course, he might perhaps have gained a triumph for his own arms, certainly have saved France from an immense catastrophe.

While Grouchy was proceeding on his ill-starred march. Napoleon had been making the grand attack on Wellington's left and left centre.

★★★★★★

While Ney and D'Erlon had been making the grand attack, ending, we have seen, in a complete reverse, disastrous intelligence had reached Napoleon. He had received the letter written by Grouchy from Walhain at eleven in the morning, which informed his master that Blücher was falling back on Brussels; that the mass of the Prussian army was being probably concentrated in the plains of the Chyse, to the north-east of Wavre and towards Louvain; and that the restraining wing would attack Wavre, but not until late in the afternoon, and would stand at that place between Blücher and Wellington, supposed to be in retreat on Brussels. This despatch, utterly opposed to the facts, proved that Grouchy had marched with extraordinary slowness from Gembloux, and was not nearly in contact with the enemy, now, known to be in part at Wavre, in part at St. Lambert;[44] that Blücher had gained several miles on Grouchy; and that the chances were faint that, even if Grouchy should draw near the main army by Moustier and Ottignies, he could be in a position to fall on Bülow's flank and rear, as both Napoleon and Soult thought would be the case when the postscript to the letter of one in the afternoon was written.

It seemed probable, on the contrary, from Grouchy's language, that the Marshal would march to Wavre as slowly as he had marched to Walhain; that he would not be at Wavre until the evening of the day; and that he might even diverge towards the plains of the Chyse, hoping still to interpose between the allied commanders, who in his view

---

44. Comment. v.: '*L'Empereur reçut de Gembloux des nouvelles bien fâcheuses. Le Maréchal Grouchy, au lieu d'être parti de Gembloux à la pointe du jour, comme il l'avait annoncé par sa dépêche de deux heures après minuit, n'avait pas encore quitté ce camp à dix heures du matin. L'officier l'attribuait à l'horrible temps qu'il faisait; motif ridicule.*' Gembloux is a mistake for Sart les Walhain, and two in the morning should be three; but Napoleon's disappointment appears plainly.

were making for Brussels.

It had become evident, therefore, to Napoleon that his lieutenant was on a wrong, possibly a fatal, course; that he must now expect that Bülow would be free to march against the right flank of the main French army, while this was attacking Wellington in front; that this diversion must be grave, and might become most perilous, and that it must be resisted, and if possible baffled. Simultaneously the Emperor was made aware by Marbot's horsemen and those of Domon that Bülow was moving from St. Lambert, and was making his way towards the Bois de Paris, a piece of woodland about a mile from the extreme French right, and about two from Plancenoit, near the French rear, and that an attack from this direction might be ere long expected.

******

It was now between five and six o'clock; the attack of Bülow had become formidable in the extreme. Half of that General's corps had not come into line at St. Lambert until near one; the other half not until after three. It was well that Grouchy was far distant. Blücher had joined his lieutenant long before this time.

******

It was now near seven o'clock in the evening; the battle was in no sense decided. Fortune cast on Napoleon a cruel smile. The attack of Bülow seemed completely spent; his columns had almost disappeared from the scene; the cannon of Grouchy at a distance was distinctly heard; the Marshal would surely hold the rest of the Prussian army in check. Blücher, as the Emperor continued to believe, with the obstinate conviction that sometimes possessed his mind, would not dare to advance from Wavre in force. In front Wellington's line had been greatly thinned and weakened; the reserves of the Duke could be hardly descried; the great main road to Brussels was choked with terror-stricken fugitives.

******

We may glance for a moment at the state of the battle while Napoleon was preparing his final attack....... And, we repeat. Napoleon at this crisis believed that Bülow had not the means to attack again. The cannon of Grouchy seemed approaching with increasing roar. Napoleon was convinced that his lieutenant would assuredly prevent the rest of the Prussian army from reaching the field. The Emperor had played his last card with fatal results. Grouchy never came.

******

After the battle Napoleon set off for Charleroy, and, passing the

Sambre, reached Philippeville in the forenoon of June 19. From that place he wrote to his brother Joseph, informing him of the disaster of the day before, and expressing a hope that he would receive the support of the nation; in a short time he had set off for Paris. He has been blamed severely for this conduct; detractors have said that 'he was a deserter, as he had been in Egypt and in 1812.' But the Emperor had, for the moment, nothing to do on the frontier; he literally was without an army; he had to think of the Chambers of Paris, of a terrified France, too willing, perhaps, to make him a victim. During the agony of the hours he had just gone through, his self-contained composure had once given way. It has been recorded by an eye-witness, that at Quatre Bras Napoleon turned his eyes towards Waterloo; silent tears trickled down cheeks almost lifeless, and pallid as if with the look of death.

We pass on to the operations of Grouchy, the paramount cause of this immense disaster for France. We left the ill-fated Marshal at Walhain, having set at nought the admirable counsels of Gérard, to cross the Dyle as quickly as possible by Moustier and Ottignies, and to march to the sound of the great fight at Waterloo. He had resolved to continue the movement on Wavre by the direct roads on the eastern bank of the river—that is, many miles away from his master. By this time, Excelmans, we have seen, had been for some time at La Baraque; Vandamme and most of his corps had reached Nil St. Vincent; they were, therefore, at a short distance from Wavre; the corps of Gérard was round Walhain and Sart les Walhain; Pajol and Teste were between Grand Leez and Tourinnes—that is, a few miles eastward.

The march of the army remained slow; and Grouchy, fixed as his purpose was, was affected by the thunder of the distant battle, and by the evident disapprobation of his own soldiery. He approached the Dyle more than once in person; but he still persisted in his fatal course; he actually withdrew squadrons of Excelmans from a place called La Plaquerie, only a few hundred yards from the bridge on the Dyle at Ottignies, Excelmans having assumed that Grouchy was about to cross the river and to push on to Waterloo and join his master.

By this time Ledebur, charged to observe Grouchy at Mont St. Guibert, and who, we have said, had not perceived the advance of the French, was almost surrounded by the Marshal's army; but he succeeded in effecting his escape to Wavre, after a short skirmish with the troops of Excelmans and Vandamme; he had received some assistance from part of the corps of Pirch, which soon afterwards resumed its march towards Waterloo, but was too late to take part in the battle. Between three and four, Grouchy, now near Wavre, received the despatch written by Soult at ten in the forenoon, which directed the Marshal, indeed, to march on Wavre, but emphatically told him he was to draw near the Emperor, about to engage in a great battle—that is, impliedly, if very obscurely, intimated that he ought to get over the Dyle, to move towards Wavre by the western bank, and, above all, to come in contact with the main army. Shallow, obstinate, and not discerning the real import of the words, Grouchy exclaimed with glee that he had done perfectly right in disregarding the advice of Gérard, and took credit to himself for his skilful strategy. But Gérard, if we are to believe Zenowicz, the bearer of the despatch, with true insight, caught Soult's meaning, and, breaking out into passion, vehemently said to Grouchy: 'If we are lost, the guilt will lie at your door!'[45]

Grouchy, satisfied with himself, and blind in his conceit, now ordered Vandamme to press on to Wavre, and to make a vigorous attack on the town; the corps of Gérard was to second the movement. His fixed idea was to fall on the enemy at hand. He did not wholly neglect the injunctions of Soult—to approach the Emperor and the main French army; but he committed this charge to Pajol and Teste—that is, to the very body of men which was farthest from the Dyle—and could not be over the river for a considerable time.

Vandamme and Excelmans, with Gérard not far in the rear, were around Wavre at about half-past four. By this time Bülow was thundering on Napoleon's right flank; Pirch, with half of his corps, was on his way to join him, between Wavre and St. Lambert; Zieten was at a short distance from Ohain, making for Waterloo. Grouchy had let the mass of the Prussian army elude his grasp; it was in full march to join hands with Wellington. The restraining wing had failed to fulfil its task. Grouchy was merely striking at the tail, so to speak, of the enemy, not falling on his side, not assailing his head, not even standing between the hostile armies. Thielmann had for some hours been left at Wavre with not more than 21,000 men.[46]

He had been informed, probably between one and two, that Grouchy was marching towards him in largely superior force, and had sent to St. Lambert to seek orders; he was curtly told by Gneisenau, or perhaps by Blücher, that everything depended on what was being

---

45. See Thiers, *Histoire du Consulat at de l'Empire*, vi. Thiers knew Gérard well, and probably had this from Gérard himself.
46. Thielmann's corps, after Ligny, was about 18,000 strong; but he had the support at Wavre of some troops of Zieten, and perhaps of Pirch, left behind.

done at Waterloo, and that he must shift for himself as well as he could. He gave up all idea of moving towards his chief, and hastily placed Wavre in a state of defence, barricading the bridges of the town on the Dyle, throwing obstacles of all kinds across the streets, crenellating houses and other buildings to secure points of vantage. In this position, one of considerable strength, he steadily awaited his enemy's attack.

Vandamme was not slow in falling on. He assailed Wavre from the eastern bank of the Dyle, and mastered the suburbs on that side; but the single division he engaged was unable to cross the stream, and was decimated by a heavy fire from the town. Meanwhile, a little after five o'clock, Grouchy had received the message from Soult, written at one, directing him once more to move towards the main army, and also the postscript ordering him to attack Bülow, as Soult and Napoleon believed he could do.[47] What must have been the thoughts of the conscience-stricken chief when the bandage had fallen at last from his eyes?

Yet Grouchy, even at this supreme moment—not that any effort of his could now have had real effect—conducted his operations with remarkable want of judgement. He, indeed, sent Pajol and Teste, by this time at hand, to seize the bridge on the Dyle at Limale, and to hasten to the western bank of the river; but he permitted Vandamme still to waste his forces in attacks on Wavre that could have no object; he did not order Vandamme to support Teste or Pajol. At the same time, he directed a single division of Gérard to assail Wavre near Biérges higher up the Dyle, and so to support the efforts of Vandamme, as if Wavre was still his main object. Gérard fell severely wounded in a fruitless attack, and it was not until Pajol and Teste had got over the Dyle that Grouchy ordered the two other divisions of Gérard to follow, and to pass over to the western bank.

The Marshal now made towards Napoleon's army; but it was past nine, and the attempt could have come to nothing—Napoleon and his army had succumbed. Thielmann, too, held Grouchy in check for a time; and though he was compelled to retreat some distance, the French were detained in positions almost around Wavre. It was eleven at night before all fighting ceased. The attacks of Vandamme had meanwhile failed; the Prussians continued masters of the town; Grouchy and Thielmann had their bivouacs between Wavre and Rixensart.

---

47. This momentous despatch, like much of Soult's work, was scribbled in pencil, and could hardly be deciphered.

The cannon of Waterloo had long been voiceless. The unfortunate Marshal clung to a hope that his master—the rumour had so run—was a victor; but Gérard, wounded, it was feared, to death, was convinced that the result had been very different. Ten miles away the truth was revealed in an appalling spectacle of wide-spread carnage, on which night spread a funereal pall. Wellington had lost more than 15,000 men, Blücher very nearly 7,000. Each had dearly paid for their great triumph. But the French army had been virtually blotted out: from 30,000 to 40,000 men had been killed, wounded, or made prisoners; from 8,000 to 10,000 were deserting; more than 200 guns had been abandoned in the rout; in all probability 30,000 men of the ruined host were never under arms again.[48]

★★★★★★

The attack on Hougoumont had been ill-conducted; that of D'Erlon had completely failed. But the allied army had been greatly weakened; it could not have resisted a combined effort made by Lobau, the French cavalry, and the Imperial Guard. In this event Wellington's left would probably have been turned and his centre forced, according to the Emperor's design; in a word, the Duke would have suffered a real defeat, but not, as we think, the overwhelming reverse which might have happened at Ligny or on June 17.[49] This peril was averted by the intervention of Bülow; his onset on Napoleon's right flank prevented the decisive movement, and in a great measure paralysed the French army. The course of the battle was completely changed, and the apparition of Zieten and Pirch on the field made Waterloo an immense victory and an immense disaster. The result of the conflict was therefore determined by the junction of Wellington's and Blücher's

---

48. For the losses of the belligerent armies at Waterloo, see Charras, ii. 67, 68; H. Houssaye, *1815 Waterloo*. The figures as regards the French army are, of course, mere conjecture; enough to say it was destroyed.

49. On this subject we agree, in substance, with Mr. Ropes, 'The Campaign of Waterloo,' 327; ' Let us suppose, then, that Napoleon could have combined his whole force against the army of Wellington during the whole afternoon; that he could have given his personal direction to the conduct of the action; that he could have followed up the repulse of the 1st corps with a new attack, in which Lobau should support D'Erlon, and in which the cavalry should take its proper part; that he had been on the spot when La Haye Sainte fell, and had improved that advantage as he well knew how to do; that he had had the whole of the Imperial Guard—infantry, cavalry, and artillery—at his disposal for the carrying of Wellington's position: it seems to us there can be no reasonable question as to the result; the Duke would have been badly beaten, and the action would, in all probability, have been over, or substantially so, by six o'clock. This question is not asked to gratify the imagination.'

forces on the same point.

Wellington fought the battle on an assurance that this would take place; Blücher had pledged himself to support his ally. The principal reason, accordingly, of the event at Waterloo was the union of the two armies in furtherance of a preconcerted plan, which crushed Napoleon by their overwhelming strength. But Napoleon had employed Grouchy to prevent this junction; he had given the Marshal a powerful restraining wing to keep Blücher away from Wellington. The question therefore arises, in considering what occurred at Waterloo: Could Grouchy, who, we know, miserably failed, have been reasonably expected to fulfil his master's purpose? Was it the more likely, having regard to the situation and the probabilities of war, that Blücher would be able to come into line with Wellington, or that Grouchy would be able to stop the veteran warrior, or even to come to Napoleon's assistance? The subject has been placed in a false light, or has been slurred over by many writers; the facts should be presented in their true aspect, and proper conclusions be drawn from them.

Undoubtedly, in the position of affairs that was witnessed on June 18, the conduct of Grouchy having been what it was, the main part of the Prussian army might have reached Waterloo at a comparatively early hour, as Wellington was convinced would be the case. Zieten and Thielmann, on the western bank of the Dyle, were considerably nearer the allied lines than Pirch and Bülow on the eastern bank. Had they been unmolested, and marched soon after daybreak, they might have been at St. Lambert, with about 25,000 men, in all probability at about ten or eleven, and have fallen on Napoleon's right flank at about twelve or one. Under similar conditions, had Pirch moved before Bülow, as his advanced position made the natural course, he could have been at St. Lambert, with perhaps 20,000 men, an hour or two probably after his colleagues; and Bülow need not have been greatly behind, assuming that he had not been kept back at Wavre with a large part of his corps, at least, to guard Blücher's communications and rear.

But in examining this question, we must consider, with reference to the matter in hand, not what the Prussian operations might have been, but what they actually were in the events that happened. Zieten and Thielmann were detained many hours at Wavre; Zieten was directed to Waterloo by the northern road through Ohain; Thielmann was kept back ultimately at Wavre the whole day in order to resist the attack of Grouchy; Bülow was moved forward before Pirch; Pirch was retarded a considerable time by the intermingling of his columns with those of Bülow. As the general result, great and unnecessary delay, apart from the obstacles that stood in its path, occurred in the movements of the Prussian army. Zieten did not break up from Wavre until about noon; he was not at Ohain until near six; he did not reach the field of battle in anything like force, and then with some 10,000 men only, until after the defeat of the Imperial Guard— that is, a short time after eight o'clock.

As for Bülow, his advanced guard was not at St. Lambert until after ten in the forenoon; his whole corps, about 29,000 strong,[50] had not reached that place until after three; he did not begin his attack until half-past four, and then with only a part of his forces. The march of Pirch was even more delayed; he did not leave Wavre until noon; two of his divisions waited for a time to observe Grouchy; he was not at Plancenoit until after eight, and then with only 12,000 or 15,000 men; his forces and those of Bülow at Waterloo were not more than from 40,000 to 45,000 men; and in the march from Wavre they were divided by long distances, and spread out into disunited columns, on a flank march of the most hazardous kind should they come within the reach of an enemy.

It should be observed, too, that, if we except Blücher, every Prussian commander gave proof of caution—nay, of timidity—in these movements. Gneisenau hesitated at the critical moment; Zieten was most reluctant to march to Papelotte, though informed that Wellington was in great danger; Bülow waited for hours before he made his attack; nay, even Blücher would not commit himself to a real effort against Napoleon until he had ascertained that his flank and rear were not threatened. The Prussian march, in a word, from Wavre to Waterloo, let the courtiers of Fortune say what they please, was ill-directed, irresolute, and dangerously delayed.

These being the uncontested facts, and the elements from which we must form our judgement, let us see whether Grouchy, giving him credit for ordinary capacity, insight, and skill, ought to have prevented the junction of Blücher and Wellington. We have indicated the operations which, beyond question, he ought to have resolved to carry out when, on the night of the 17th, he was at Gembloux with his army of 33,000 men. He had been placed at the head of a strong restraining wing; his companions in arms, and he himself likewise, must have been aware that his duty was to hold Blücher in check, while the Emperor should fall in full force on Wellington. Napoleon, when giving

---

50. Excluding the detachment of Ledebur.

him his command, had all but certainly told him not only to pursue Blücher and to keep him in sight, but also to be in constant communication with the main French army; he undoubtedly added that he meant to attack Wellington, should Wellington make a stand before the Forest of Soignies. A short time afterwards the Marshal received positive orders, through the important message despatched by Bertrand, to march on Gembloux, to follow the enemy, and to correspond with his master at headquarters; and he was distinctly warned that the allied Generals might be seeking to effect their junction, and even to fight another battle. Grouchy reached Gembloux, though very late, on the evening of the 17th.

At that place he learned, in the course of a few hours, that the Prussian army was assembled around Wavre; he wrote twice to the Emperor that he would march to that place—probably in the first letter; in the second, certainly—adding that he would try to keep the Prussians away from Wellington, a proof that he understood his mission. In the existing situation, what Grouchy ought to do was plain—he should break up from Gembloux at the earliest dawn; should march rapidly by the two available roads; should cross the Dyle by the bridges of Moustier and Ottignies, a distance of some ten miles from Gembloux; and should place his army on the western bank of the river: for by this movement, and by this alone, could he adequately perform his allotted task. Were Blücher halting at Wavre, he could attack him—perhaps most readily from the position he would have gained; were Blücher, as might be expected and feared, attempting to march from Wavre to join Wellington, Grouchy would be able to reach the Prussian army's flank, to attack it when placed in the worst conditions, and all but certainly to bring it to a stand—to defeat it in detail; above all, he would draw near Napoleon, and be soon in contact with the imperial army.[51]

Instead of making the movement the occasion required, Grouchy, we know, left Gembloux at a very late hour; marched extremely slowly to Walhain and Sart les Walhain; advanced along the eastern bank of the Dyle; persisted in this, spite of the entreaties of Gérard to cross the stream and to make for Waterloo; allowed Blücher to give him the slip, and to join Wellington with more than half his army; and, keeping many miles away from Napoleon, merely reached at Wavre the

---

51. All commentators, Jomini, Charras, Thiers, La Tour d'Auvergne, Clausewitz, H. Houssaye, Ropes, and many others, agree that this was what Grouchy should have done. See authorities collected by Mr. Ropes, *The Campaign of Waterloo*.

corps of Thielmann. But had he operated as he ought to have done, and as any true soldier would have done in his place, what he might have accomplished is hardly doubtful. On the night of the 17th Excelmans and his horsemen were between Sauvenière and Nil St. Vincent; Vandamme was a little beyond Gembloux, Gérard a little behind the town; Pajol and Teste were some miles in the rear round Mazy. Had Grouchy formed an energetic purpose to march as quickly as possible across the Dyle, he might have had the corps of Vandamme and Gérard under arms by four in the morning of June 18; he might have directed Excelmans to cover the intended movement, and Pajol and Teste to follow Excelmans without delay.

Had he taken these steps—and they were almost obvious—he might have marched to the Dyle with Vandamme and Gérard by the roads passing through Villeroux and Cortel; and if his march had been at the rate of about two miles an hour, his columns having been divided to ensure celerity, he would have reached the river between nine and ten in the forenoon at the two bridges of Moustier and Ottignies, having possibly surprised and cut to pieces the detachment of Ledebur at Mont St. Guibert—Ledebur, we have seen, was surprised in the afternoon—having certainly swept it out of his path. The bridges were of stone, and, like those on the Sambre, had, whatever the reason, been left intact. With the exception of the weak divisions of Pajol and Teste—and these would not have been far in the rear—Grouchy would have been across the Dyle and on the western bank before noon, as has been acknowledged even by the most bitter of Napoleon's detractors.[52]

Grouchy and the mass of his forces, being now over the Dyle, had two alternative courses to take; either would have given him an opportunity grand and decisive. At Moustier and Ottignies he was about six miles from Maransart, a village near Plancenoit, on the other bank of the Lasne, and some two miles from the main French army. At Moustier and Ottignies, too, he was only some three miles farther from Napoleon than Bülow at St. Lambert was; he was not more than four or five miles from the flank of the corps of Bülow, now on its march from Wavre in disunited masses, and not expecting an enemy at hand. Had Grouchy, as no doubt he would have done, pushed his cavalry forward in both directions, he would have come in contact

---

52. Jomini (*The Campaign of Waterloo 1815*) says that Grouchy would have reached Moustier at about ten. Charras (2) admits that he could have been over the Dyle 'before noon.'

almost at once with the horsemen of Marbot sent to the two bridges, and he would have ascertained how affairs stood with Bülow.

In this situation Grouchy, we are convinced, would have marched directly on Maransart in conformity with the message given by Marbot; he would have reached that place between two and three, long before Bülow had begun his attack; he would have received the Emperor's commands; in all human probability, he would have been placed either before or behind the Bois de Paris in order to cover Napoleon's right flank, and to protect it from any effort to be made by Bülow. In that event Grouchy would have interposed with complete effect between Blücher and Wellington; Bülow certainly would not have attempted to attack—at least, until he had been reinforced by Pirch, then on a march many miles in the rear; Zieten assuredly would not have stirred from Ohain; in the meantime Napoleon, left free to act with all his forces, including the Guard, would beyond question have overpowered Wellington.

Grouchy, on the march from Moustier and Ottignies, could hardly have received the despatch from Soult, sent off, we have seen, at half-past one, and directing him to fall on the flank and rear of Bülow. Conceivably, however, though not probably, he might have decided on marching against that General; in that event he would have reached the lines of Bülow's march between two and three, but his influence would have been felt long before; the Prussians would have been surprised and caught in a perilous flank march by an enemy superior in force at the decisive point. In this position they must have hesitated and paused for a time; his was inevitable, from the nature of the case; if so, Bülow's attack would have been delayed some hours. We must bear in mind that even Blücher would not run the risk until he had ascertained that his flank and rear were safe.

The attack might not have been made at all, and Pirch, in all probability, would not have moved towards Bülow with the two divisions—all he had in hand. He would, it is all but certain, have waited for his two divisions in the rear. Bülow and Pirch, in a word, would have been paralysed by the apparition on their flank of an unexpected enemy—at least not less than 30,000 strong. They could not have acted with effect for some hours. Zieten, of course, would not have stirred a step. Grouchy would have prevented Blücher from joining Wellington, and secured for Napoleon time to gain the day at Waterloo. It should be added that, had Grouchy marched against Bülow in the position in which the Prussians were, he might very possibly have annihilated part of their forces, scattered as these were, and most dangerously exposed.

These conclusions, however, as sound, we believe, as is possible in a case of the kind, have been assailed by specious, but, we think, false sophistry. The movement of Grouchy to Moustier and Ottignies would, it has been said, have been perceived by Ledebur at Mont St. Guibert; and that officer would have carried the news to Wavre, and have reached the town perhaps by eight in the morning. In that event Gneisenau and Blücher would at once have made a complete change in the dispositions of the Prussian army, and in the arrangements which had been prepared for its advance on Waterloo. Zieten, who had been directed to stay around Wavre, would have been moved to the Dyle and the bridges of Moustier and Ottignies; Pirch, who was to second the march of Bülow, would have been turned aside from the road to St. Lambert, and ordered to hold the bridges of Limale and Limelette on the Dyle.

In that case Grouchy could not have got over the river; he would have found a large army in his path; he would have at least been compelled to fight a battle, which necessarily would have detained him for hours. Under these conditions Thielmann would have been sent to support Bülow, and both would have overwhelmed Napoleon with the aid of Wellington. Nay, even if, as was not probable, Grouchy had succeeded in crossing the Dyle, the whole Prussian army would have made for Waterloo; Pirch and Zieten would have followed in the track of Grouchy; Bülow and Thielmann would have joined Wellington; Napoleon would not the less have been destroyed.[53]

This reasoning disregards important facts of the case, and is opposed to the natural inferences to be drawn in war. We may grant that Ledebur would have reached Wavre at about eight, and given news of Grouchy; if, as was most likely, he could not have had time to estimate the numbers of the Marshal's army, Blücher and Gneisenau, who, we must bear in mind, thought that Grouchy had not more than 15,000 men, and were making preparations to join Wellington, would assuredly have made no changes in these, and would not have sent Zieten and Pirch to the Dyle: for this, from their point of view, would have been a false movement.

If, on the contrary, Ledebur had ascertained that Grouchy was at the head of some 30,000 men, and was making for the Dyle by Moustier and Ottignies, it is equally certain that not one of the movements that

---

53. Charras, 2.

have been suggested would have been made. Eager as Blücher was to push on to Waterloo, Gneisenau, his strategic mentor and master, was at this very time in hesitation as to whether the march should be made. He was craning, so to speak, like a hunter at a fence. If he had learned, to his surprise and amazement, how formidable was the power of Grouchy's force, he would very probably have detained the whole Prussian army around Wavre—the foremost column of Bülow was still at hand—and not moved for two or three hours at least, until the situation had developed itself. In that event Grouchy would have had ample time to advance across the Dyle, and to join Napoleon; not a single division of the Prussian army would have reached Waterloo until it was far too late to give the slightest support to Wellington; the defeat of Wellington would have been assured.

It may be admitted, however, having regard to Blücher's heroic nature and high sense of honour, that the old chief would have insisted that no change should be made in the arrangements for the march on Waterloo, and that, though made aware of the real strength of Grouchy, he would have ordered Bülow, Pirch, and Zieten to continue their projected movements. But in that case Grouchy, as we have seen, would have been able to reach Maransart, or to arrest the advance of Bülow and Pirch, and therefore of Zieten; in other words, he would have prevented Blücher from joining Wellington; Waterloo would have been a victory for France.

As to the supposition that, when it had become known that Grouchy was close to the Dyle with a real and large army, Zieten and Pirch would have been sent to stop him upon the river, and, still more, that the whole Prussian army would have been directed to follow the Marshal, and to press on to Waterloo, it may confidently be said that such an operation was never conducted in war. Were there no other reason, the Prussian commanders would never have left Wavre without a considerable force to protect their communications and rear.[54]

Had Grouchy, therefore, got over the Dyle at Moustier and Ottignies by the forenoon, he would have accomplished his master's purpose, and kept Blücher away from Wellington. Let us next consider what he might have achieved had he, giving ear to the counsels of Gérard, marched from Walhain on Waterloo on hearing the roar of the battle. At this moment—that is, not far from noon—the cavalry of Excelmans had reached La Baraque, a point about three miles from

---

54. For an able refutation of the arguments of Charras on this subject, see Ropes, *The Campaign of Waterloo*.

the Dyle; part of the corps of Vandamme was at Nil St.Vincent, the remaining part being not far behind. Gérard and his corps were at Walhain and Sart les Walhain; Pajol and Teste were approaching Tourinnes. These distances were between six and eight miles from the river. Had Grouchy, therefore, marched to the Dyle, and crossed it at the bridges of Moustier and Ottignies, sending Excelmans and Vandamme to the nearest bridges at Limale and Limelette—these, like the others, were of stone, and not broken—he would have been over the river about four, the divisions of Pajol and Teste remaining on the eastern bank, and covering, as Gérard had proposed, the movement.

At this time Bülow had not fired a shot; two of his divisions were in the defiles of the Lasne. Only half of the corps of Pirch was much beyond Wavre; it did not reach Plancenoit until long after eight. Zieten was still a march of two hours from Ohain. Thielmann was encamped in and around Wavre. In these circumstances Grouchy, of course, would have pushed forward, his march accelerated by the sound of the cannon; and he would have made his influence felt at once on Bülow and Pirch, for he would be on their flank only three or four miles distant, just as Bülow made his influence felt with effect on Napoleon from St. Lambert, about as far from the French army.

Bülow and Pirch must have paused and made preparations to resist an attack; both, especially the first, were in a position that might become most critical. It may be confidently said that Bülow's attack on Napoleon would have been long postponed; and had it then been made, it would have been too late; Napoleon would have been master of the field at Waterloo. The march of Bülow, in a word, must have been arrested; that of Pirch and Zieten would have equally come to a stand. No doubt, possibly, but not probably, Thielmann would have advanced from Wavre to support Pirch; but the result would practically have been the same. Grouchy, though outnumbered, would have been able to detain the Prussians on their march sufficiently long to give the Emperor the means of defeating Wellington. It ought to be added that, as Gérard has maintained. Grouchy not improbably would have succeeded in destroying parts of the corps of Pirch and Bülow, surprised and caught in a position of no little peril.

The kind of argument, however, which has been employed to prove that Grouchy could not have kept Blücher and Wellington apart, had he crossed the Dyle by the early forenoon, has been urged to show that had Grouchy, at Walhain, followed the advice of Gérard to march on Waterloo, the result would, even more certainly, have been the same. Ledebur, it is said, would have reported to Wavre the movement of the French army to the Dyle, which he would have seen long before it reached the stream; the corps of Thielmann, and part of the corps of Pirch—these, it will be recollected, still near Wavre—would have been directed to the bridges to stop the march of the enemy. Grouchy would, therefore, be compelled to fight a battle; this must have detained him until nightfall. He could not even have drawn near Napoleon, still less have prevented the junction of Blücher and Wellington. Besides, time and distance, though no Prussians had stood in the Marshal's path, would have made it impossible for him to do anything to assist his master or to molest the allies; he could not have crossed the Dyle until about six, or have reached the field of battle until nine or ten. At that hour the French army was in complete rout; he probably would have been involved in the general ruin.[55]

These arguments, we think, are even more unsound than those we have already dealt with. Ledebur completely failed to perceive the movement of the French on La Baraque and Nil St. Vincent; he did not stir from Mont St. Guibert until after one. He was surprised and all but cut off; he could not have reached Wavre until between three and four. There is no reason to suppose that he would have been more vigilant, have acted differently, and have done better, had Grouchy marched to the bridges on the Dyle; if so, any report he could have made at Wavre would have been much too late to enable a large Prussian force to move to the bridges in order to stop Grouchy. Besides, Thielmann, who by this time must have ascertained that Grouchy was at the head of an army more than twice as numerous as had been supposed, and who had been just ordered to defend the town, would never have attempted to leave Wavre; and the half of the corps of Pirch, which had remained in the rear, and was even now marching to join the other half, would not have been diverted from its movement on St. Lambert to make an attempt to hold Grouchy in check on the Dyle.

As to time and distance, the arguments are either false in fact or point to conclusions plainly erroneous. Grouchy would have been over the Dyle long before six; once he was across, the question would not have been at what hour his army would have reached Waterloo, but when it would have made its power so felt by the Prussians as to arrest and prevent their attack on Napoleon. That influence would have told, and told with effect, almost as soon as the Marshal had

---

55. Charras, 2.

crossed the Dyle. An army threatening another upon a hazardous flank march, especially as affairs stood with Bülow and Pirch, would paralyse it long before it could strike it; and that being so, Grouchy could have stopped his enemy. We fully acknowledge, however, that Grouchy's movement in the afternoon could not have had the decisive effect his movement in the morning would have had; it might have enabled Napoleon to employ the whole Imperial Guard, but could not have prevented the wasteful and unsuccessful cavalry attacks.[56]

It is unnecessary to notice the idle remark that, as Grouchy was ordered to march to Wavre, he is not to be blamed for not making a different movement, however better this might have been. Napoleon and perhaps Soult are alone to blame.[57] Writers who take this position are blind to the facts, or worse. Apart from the interpretation to be put on Soult's letters, Grouchy did not receive these until the afternoon of the 18th; his instructions were those given by Napoleon on the 17th, either in person or through the message of Bertrand. He was perfectly free to march to Moustier and Ottignies from four in the morning of the 18th to four in the evening; he is solely responsible for not having taken this course. Another criticism on Grouchy of very different value is of real importance, and deserves close attention.

Since the publication of Marbot's *Memoirs*, Napoleon, we know, expected Grouchy to cross the Dyle at Moustier and Ottignies, and to be on the field of Waterloo at an early hour, whether in compliance or not with orders received on the night of the 17th, which were given, we believe, but never reached the Marshal. Apart, however, from considerations of this kind, Napoleon, in his narrative of the campaign, has pronounced a judgement on Grouchy's conduct, and on what he might have done on June 17 and 18, which cannot be lightly passed over. Grouchy, we have seen, had marched extremely slowly to Gembloux; had halted around the town on the night of the 17th; had left his camp very late on the following day, and had only reached Wavre about half-past four, soon before he began his attack on Thielmann.

The Emperor has insisted that had his lieutenant advanced beyond

---

56. As to the operations of Grouchy and to what he might have accomplished, the reader may be referred to Jomini, *The Campaign of Waterloo 1815;* Thiers, *Histoire du Consulat et de l'Empire,* vi.; Van Loben Sels, 322, 323, 340; La Tour d'Auvergne, *Waterloo;* Ropes, *The Waterloo Campaign;* H. Houssaye, *1815 Waterloo.* The only writer who takes a contrary view, and has dealt with the subject seriously, is Charras (2). He is able and plausible, but inaccurate and sophistical. No English writer has gone really into the question.

57. Mr. Ropes (*The Campaign of Waterloo*) has treated this criticism as it deserves.

Gembloux to Wavre on the 17th, or had marched rapidly and early on the 18th, and had been before Wavre in the forenoon, he would either have kept the whole of Blücher's army on the spot, or three-fourths of it—that is, excepting the corps of Bülow; and in either event the French would have gained Waterloo.[58] We may think that, in coming to this conclusion, Napoleon underrated Blücher's energy, and that the Prussian army, 90,000 strong, or three-fourths of it, would not have been completely held in check by Grouchy, appearing with only 33,000 men, at Wavre; the movement could not have been as effective as that across the Dyle by Moustier and Ottignies, which would have brought Grouchy on the flank of Bülow and Pirch, far from each other and in divided masses. But if we bear in mind that Blücher and Gneisenau thought that Grouchy had only 15,000 men, it is very difficult to say that, when they had ascertained he had a force before Wavre of more than two-fold strength, they would not have kept the greatest part of the Prussian army around the town for hours, and thus given time to Napoleon to defeat Wellington.

Had Grouchy, therefore, been worthy of his trust, the facts and the probabilities of the case show that he could have prevented the junction of Blücher and Wellington, and secured a victory for his master on June 18.[59] The question was not, as has been untruly said, of the superiority in numbers of the Prussian army; it was whether, as affairs stood on the scene of events, the French restraining wing had the means to stop it, and this can be answered in the affirmative with but little room for doubt. It follows that Grouchy was the real and the main author of the disaster that befell the arms of France; the Marshal's conduct. Napoleon has justly remarked, was no more to be anticipated than that an earthquake would swallow up his whole army on his march.[60]

---

58. *Comment.*, v.: '*Si le Maréchal Grouchy eût couché devant Wavre, comme il le devait et eu reçut l'ordre le soir du 17, le Maréchal Blücher y fût resté en observation, avec toutes ses forces; se croyant poursuivi par toute l'armée française. Si le Maréchal Grouchy comme il l'avait écrit à deux heures après minuit de son camp à Gembloux, eût pris les armes à la pointe du jour, c'est à dire à quatre heures du matin, il ne fût pas arrivé à Wavre à temps pour empêcher le détachement du Général Bülow, mais il eût arrêté les trois autres corps du Général Blücher; la victoire était encore certaine.*'

59. Jomini (*The Campaign of Waterloo 1815*) pointedly says: '*Le plan d'opérations adopté était si bien le plus convenable, que . . . il eût complètement réussi . . . si l'aile droite avail pris la direction de Moustier.*'

60. *Comment.* v.: '*La conduite du Maréchal Grouchy était aussi imprévoyable que si, sur sa route, son armée eût éprouvé un tremblement de terre qui l'eût engloutie.*'

But it does not follow that the Emperor was altogether free from blame, though this is infinitely less than has been commonly supposed. The lethargy which made him prostrate on the morning of the 17th explains, and can alone explain, how it came to pass that the line of Blücher's retreat was not ascertained at an early hour, and Grouchy not detached with the restraining wing to hold the Prussian army so completely in check that it could not by any possibility reach that of Wellington. But for this Napoleon would deserve the severest censure; as the facts are, he is more to be pitied than condemned.

We believe, too, that the Emperor, on the night of the 17th, did communicate with Grouchy more frequently than has been acknowledged by most of his critics; it seems most probable that he ordered the Marshal to move on Waterloo with a detachment or with his whole army, though Grouchy never received the message. But Napoleon underrated Blücher, and was too obstinately convinced that the veteran at Wavre could not draw near Wellington—though even here we must recollect the Bertrand letter; he turned a deaf ear to the warnings of Jerôme, perhaps of Milhaud; he placed too implicit a faith in Grouchy, and refused to see that an army of 90,000 men might elude an army of 33,000 if this was not directed by an able chief. Napoleon, too, ought to have been more observant of the despatches of Soult—ambiguous, ill-worded, sent often by a single officer too late; but here again he deserves rather compassion than blame. Perhaps his chief fault was that he gave Grouchy a command, which he ought to have seen that Grouchy was not fit for, from the Marshal's own expressions on the 17th; had Gérard had the command of the restraining wing, the catastrophe that was witnessed would not have occurred.

As it was most probable that Grouchy would possess the means of separating Blücher from Wellington on June 18, it follows, too, that the movement of Blücher to join Wellington was perilous and essentially bad strategy, and of this Gneisenau appears to have been conscious. Had the Prussian Generals been aware that Grouchy was at hand with 33,000 men, very possibly they would not have stirred from Wavre—for some time, at least; but, with Wellington, they believed he had only 15,000. Yet it is astonishing they entertained this idea; they ought to have been convinced, from a study of Napoleon's campaigns, that he would detach a powerful restraining wing to keep them away from Wellington while the Emperor should fall on the army at Waterloo. Nevertheless, they made the movement, being in ignorance of the real facts.

This secured a decisive and grand triumph, but it ought to have been rendered vain by Grouchy; and then the errors of this combination would have become apparent, the Prussian army would have been placed in the gravest danger, and Wellington would have certainly lost the battle. It has been truly said, besides, that the projects of the allied leaders were such as ought to have ensured their defeat. Had Grouchy had only 15,000 men with him. Napoleon would have been able to attack the Duke with not much less than 100,000; his army could not have escaped a disaster at Waterloo. And this brings us back to what we have said before—Wellington, as affairs stood, ought not to have fought on the 18th; the probabilities were far too distinctly against him. No doubt he expected the Prussians to be on the field much sooner than they were; but he believed that Napoleon was before him with nearly 100,000 men, all excellent troops of one nation. He had not more than 70,000 of many races—a third, at least, not good.

What chances would he have had without the support of Blücher, on which he could not reckon with reasonable hope? Nay, what chances would he have had, spite of Grouchy's faults had the Emperor attacked him in the early morning? Beyond question, as Napoleon has proved, he ought to have retreated beyond Brussels, and effected there his junction with Blücher; both would then have been assured of ultimate success, neither would have well-nigh courted defeat. That Wellington did not adopt this obvious course was probably because he thought the retention of Brussels of the highest importance to the allied cause; he sacrificed military to political ends, very seldom judicious conduct in war.

To extol the strategy of the allies on June 17 and 18 is simply to set the plainest evidence at naught. But national prejudice is of enormous power; the idolaters of success, the detractors of genius, were to act according to their ignoble kind. Hence the operations of Grouchy have been misdescribed—nay, falsified—or, what is worse, have been little noticed, though obviously of supreme importance. It was necessary to justify the ill-designed movement from Ligny to Wavre, a half-measure that ought to have been disastrous. Attempts have therefore been made to prove that, whatever Grouchy could do, this made the movement of Blücher on Waterloo certain. It was necessary to maintain the absurd position that the allies outmanoeuvred Napoleon on the 17th and the 18th. It has been contended, accordingly, that the great master never even suspected the plans of his enemies; that he sent Grouchy in the wrong direction; that he did not conceive it was

Grouchy's duty to keep Blücher away from Wellington at any point in the space between Wavre and Waterloo—nay, to be in close relations with the main French army.

It was necessary, in order to support these views, to make charges against Napoleon which cannot be sustained, and to make apologies for Grouchy that are utterly untrue; to insist that the Emperor scarcely gave a thought to the position of his lieutenant, and that it was for him to do what Grouchy was bound to do—to ascertain accurately where the Prussians were; to show that Grouchy could not on June 18 have stopped—nay, even delayed—Blücher; to make the Emperor alone responsible for the defeat of Waterloo; to exonerate the Marshal wholly from blame. Especially it was necessary to hurry over the facts; to avoid a thorough investigation of them; to jump to the conclusion that, because Blücher was largely superior in force, it was impossible that Grouchy could act with effect against him; to deal in plausible generalities; to avoid sound criticism. This sophistry and mystification, however, are being dispelled; few capable writers will now deny that, but for Grouchy, Napoleon would have gained Waterloo, and that the allies, many and great as their merits were, ought not to have been victorious on June 18.[61]

******

The Emperor on the night of the 15th was suffering from the physical decline which affected his conduct in the campaign, but we differ from the critics who impute inactivity to him on the morning of the 16th. He thought his enemies were falling back before him, according to true strategic principles; there was no necessity, in that case, for a rapid forward movement. He expected easily to master Quatre Bras and Sombreffe, and even to reach Brussels on June 17. But his dispositions were so ably made that they assured him success in almost any event, and ought to have secured him decisive success in the events that happened. Ney was directed to occupy Quatre Bras, and to send a detachment to his right to support the main army; Grouchy was ordered to advance to Sombreffe, and even to Gembloux.

---

61. For a general review and criticism of the combinations of the allies on June 17 and 18, see the unanswerable remarks of Napoleon, *Comment.* v.. The Emperor's figures are far from correct, but his reasoning and the conclusions he draws are irresistible. No real attempt has been made to refute them. Mr. Ropes (*The Campaign of Waterloo*) substantially accepts them. We have accepted them also, but with some reservations. German and English writers as a rule avoid a thorough examination of the subject.

But meanwhile Blücher had pressed forward to Sombreffe and Ligny with three-fourths of his army only, eager to give battle, hoping for aid from Wellington, who, however, was in no position to give it. Napoleon admirably seized the occasion, and made arrangements that ought to have destroyed the Prussian army—nay, probably brought the campaign to an end. While the Emperor should attack Blücher in front, the detachment of Ney was to fall on his rear; D'Erlon was ordered afterwards to make a similar movement. Had either attack been made, Ligny would have been another Jena.

✶✶✶✶✶✶

But all went wrong with the French army on that eventful night; the retreat of the Prussians was not even observed. Napoleon fell ill, and was overcome by the lethargy that for a time paralysed his commanding powers. He gave no orders until late on the morning of the 17th; he even contemplated a halt for a day. As the forenoon was advancing, he changed his purpose; he gave Grouchy a large restraining wing, directing him to follow Blücher and to complete his defeat, warning him that the allied leaders might try to unite, practically ordering the Marshal to stand between them. He then marched to Quatre Bras with the mass of his forces, in the hope of reaching and overpowering Wellington. This was his characteristic and perfectly correct strategy, but it was too late; the opportunity had been lost. Napoleon had again to complain of Ney at Quatre Bras, but the chance of completely defeating Wellington had passed away; the Duke had skilfully effected his retreat. Napoleon pursued his adversary, but to little purpose; military movements were almost prevented by torrents of rain. The French army on the evening of the 17th halted in front of Wellington's army before Waterloo.

✶✶✶✶✶✶

Meanwhile Grouchy, in command of the restraining wing, had reached Gembloux, where he had been sent by Napoleon; but his movement had been extraordinarily slow. On the night of the 17th he was hardly beyond Gembloux—that is, from ten to fourteen miles from Wavre. This was a bad beginning; but nothing was yet endangered had Grouchy taken his measures for the next day with judgement and insight. He had ascertained long before daybreak on the 18th that the Prussian army was around Wavre; had he broken up from Gembloux at an early hour, and marched across the Dyle by Moustier and Ottignies, he would have prevented Blücher from joining Wellington, and France would not have lost Waterloo.

The morning of June 18 has come; the decisive success which might have been won on the 16th and the 17th is now hardly possible. Napoleon, indeed, might have been checkmated. Had the allied commanders fallen back beyond Brussels, they could have joined hands without running risks; in that case their armies would have been greatly superior to the French in numbers. Napoleon would have been fortunate had he repassed the frontier—discomfited, baffled, his plans frustrated. But Wellington chose to make a stand at Waterloo with an army weaker than it need have been, and very much weaker than that of his enemy, on the assumption that Blücher would come to his support, about mid-day or a little after.

The Duke believed that Napoleon had more than 90,000 men in his front, the whole French army, in fact, except 15,000; he could not have withstood the Emperor's attack, in that case, for any length of time with his motley army of 70,000. Nay, though Napoleon had only 72,000 men, the Duke would have been defeated before his colleague could reach him, had the attack been made in the early forenoon, as it would have certainly been made but for the state of the weather. On the other hand, neither Blücher nor Wellington had a right to suppose that a powerful restraining wing would not be employed to prevent their junction; in that position of affairs they had no right to assume that their armies would come together on the field of the battle at hand.

These calculations were in principle false; it was the insolent play of fortune that they proved successful. The great fight of Waterloo, however, begins; the tactics of the French show impatience and want of caution; the attacks are ill-conducted and ill-designed. Ney is as reckless as he was remiss at Quatre Bras; the strength of Napoleon's army is wasted. The defence of Wellington is most admirably sustained; the constancy of his British and German Legionary troops is above praise. Meanwhile Grouchy, the commander of the restraining wing, does exactly what he ought not to do; he leaves Gembloux late; his movements are slow. He does not make for the Dyle at Moustier and Ottignies; he sets at naught the counsels of Gérard, and will not march on Waterloo when he hears its thunder. He does not try to place himself between Blücher and Wellington; he advances to Wavre, keeping aloof from his master; he allows Blücher, scarcely molested, to reach the decisive scene of action.

The restraining wing, in a word, is almost worse than useless. Meantime Bülow begins his attack. Napoleon is compelled to fight two battles; the French army is placed in terrible straits; and, after the defeat of part of the Imperial Guard, the irruption of Zieten and Pirch completes a disaster almost as frightful as ever was seen in war. But had Grouchy been equal to his task, the catastrophe could not have occurred; nay, Waterloo would have been a victory for the arms of France.

The splendour of the triumph achieved at Waterloo cannot hide from the sight of the true student of war the strategic errors which, so to speak, were its prelude. The superiority of Napoleon in the great combinations of his art, and the complete inferiority of his opponents, are, indeed, the salient features of the campaign of 1815; these give it its chief historical interest. With an army not much more than half in numbers that of his enemy, the Emperor outmanoeuvres the allied commanders at once; but for accidents he would have routed Blücher on the 16th, and probably routed Wellington on the next day. His chances on the 18th were less; but he would have gained Waterloo had he attacked in the morning, or had Gérard had the command of Grouchy. The strategy of his adversaries, on the other hand, was essentially faulty from first to last; strategically they were not fit to cope with Napoleon. Their arrangements before the contest were ill-conceived; the dispersion of their forces, the weakness of their centre, the great distance between their headquarters, their immobility when they first heard of Napoleon's advance—all this subjected them from the outset to the gravest peril.

Other and even more palpable mistakes followed. Blücher rushed into the lion's mouth at Ligny, and only escaped being swallowed up by a chance. The delays of Wellington on the 15th may be yet explained; but they were unfortunate in a very high degree. The campaign might have been brought to an end at Ligny. Gneisenau's march to Wavre was a bad half-measure, which increased the distance between the allied armies; the Duke ought not to have left a great detachment at Hal and Tubize, and weakened his army at the decisive point. He ought not to have offered battle on the 18th; the flank march from Wavre ought to have failed—nay, proved disastrous. Blücher and Wellington, instead of running enormous and unnecessary risks, ought to have fallen behind Brussels, and thus have baffled their enemy, and made their ultimate success certain.

★★★★★★

We can only ascribe the extraordinary failure of that day, when the issue of the contest was virtually in his hands, to the lethargy which occasionally made him prostrate, and simply good for nothing. He would have gained Waterloo but for the strange misconduct of Grouchy, an aberration of judgement most difficult to account for. He could even have won but for the state of the weather. The paramount causes of the result of the campaign were that Napoleon was not the Napoleon of old, and that the lieutenants in whom he trusted failed him. Soult, too, the Chief of his Staff, deserves severe censure for his inactivity, his remissness, and bad despatches. Very possibly he had much to do with the tissue of mistakes that kept Grouchy away from his master.[62] Except Gérard, too, the subordinate chiefs of the French army were inferior to their former selves, and this was especially the case with the chiefs in the highest command.

Nor can this surprise anyone acquainted with the facts. The memory of past misfortunes weighed heavily on all these men. They were unnerved by the prospect of a struggle with Europe; they had been demoralised by the events of 1814-15; they were divided by jealousies and angry discords; they knew their officers and their troops had little confidence in them. The contest may be described in a figure of speech: the eagle was suffering, even when it made its swoop. This, at the outset, was terrible and swift; but it could not use its wings to close on its quarry; it had to fight with beak and talons only; and yet it was with difficulty overpowered by the birds of prey that gathered around it at last.

✶✶✶✶✶✶

The rout of Waterloo left the army of Grouchy the only organised force remaining to France in Belgium. The Marshal, ignorant of the catastrophe, cherished, we have seen, the illusion that his master had won the battle; he resolved during the night of June 18 to make good his way from Wavre to Brussels, where he expected to find and join the main French army. He ordered Vandamme to cross the Dyle and to come into line with him, and made preparations for a determined attack on the enemy in his front between Rixensart and Wavre. By daybreak on the 19th Thielmann received the news that the allies had gained a decisive victory; he detached a considerable part of his troops to the support of Zieten, who, we have said, had not reached Waterloo in force—it is difficult to understand this movement; he fell on Grouchy at an early hour in the morning, assuming that the Marshal was thinking only of his escape.

---

62. Thiébault, we have said, disliked Soult, but says of the Marshal (*Mémoires*, v.); '*Bourmont major-général n'eut pas mieux fait que Soult.*'

Grouchy, however, had as yet heard nothing of the tragical events which had just taken place; he made a vigorous resistance, but was compelled to give way, Vandamme having disobeyed his orders, and not having come to his superior's aid. The Prussians pressed forward, Thielmann having been informed of the results of Waterloo by a despatch from Blücher himself, and having been apprised that Pirch had been sent off from the field to intercept Grouchy and to bar his retreat. But the French successfully opposed the enemy; and part of Vandamme's corps having reached the scene, Thielmann was obliged to execute a change of front, this, however, enabling him still to keep Grouchy in check, and to retain his hold on the roads from Wavre to Brussels. But Grouchy, seconded by this time by Vandamme in force, resumed the offensive and advanced. Thielmann, assailed in front, and threatened in flank by one of the divisions of Vandamme which had crossed the Dyle, with somewhat precipitate haste retreated, and, losing all contact with the allied army, fell back fully half a march towards Louvain.

It was now near eleven in the forenoon. Grouchy, still in command of more than 30,000 men—his losses at Wavre were not 3,000—pushed forward to Rosieren and La Bavette, elated with his recent success, fully expecting that he would soon meet the Emperor. At this moment a haggard spectre, so to speak, came across him. This was one of the two messengers[63] sent off to inform the unfortunate Marshal of the late catastrophe; broken down and terror-stricken, he could hardly utter a word or report his orders, which appear not to have been in writing.[64] Grouchy, doubtless stung by conscience to the quick, and shedding, it has been said, bitter tears to no purpose, instantly assembled a kind of council of war. His first and, we must add his natural, impulse was to try to justify his conduct on the preceding day, and especially to explain why he had not followed the counsels of Gérard to march on Waterloo.

His excuses were the lame and utterly false apologies which he afterwards endeavoured to palm off on history; he was listened to in cold and significant silence. The time, however, for complaining of what had happened was passed; the terrible question was before the French chiefs how to extricate themselves from the midst of their victorious enemies, and if possible to effect their retreat into France.

63. Charras (2) says there was but a single messenger. H. Houssaye (*1815 Waterloo*) says there were two—one a spy.
64. Another of the innumerable proofs of the negligence of Soult.

Grouchy thought for a moment of making an attempt to close on the rear of the hostile armies, and thus to attract them towards his own; Vandamme boldly proposed to advance on Brussels, and then, making a long circuit southwards, to reach the frontier between Lille and Valenciennes. These vain projects, however, were soon abandoned; Grouchy properly resolved to adopt the only course that promised a reasonable hope of safety—to fall back on Namur, and thence to make his way along the Meuse to Givet. It is still uncertain whether, in taking this step, he was acting in conformity to his master's orders, which seem to have indicated a movement in this direction.[65]

★★★★★★

The retreat began before noon on the 19th; it was conducted with praiseworthy celerity, and on this day with judgement. Pajol, a very skilful and experienced soldier, was despatched to observe Thielmann, and to feign pursuit; Excelmans pressed onwards to Namur with his cavalry, and reached the fortress before nightfall, a march from Wavre of more than twenty miles. Meanwhile the rest of the army retreated in two columns—Grouchy, with the corps of Gérard, by Mont St. Guibert and Gentinnes; Vandamme and his corps by Dion le Mont, Tourinnes, and Grand Leez. The movement was not molested; it was about twice as rapid as that from Gembloux to Wavre on June 18. By the close of the day Grouchy had attained the main lateral road from Nivelles to Namur, and had his bivouacs round Mazy and Temploux; Vandamme had advanced beyond Gembloux, and was but a few miles from the Marshal on his right. The double march was one of about twenty miles; it contrasts most strikingly with that of the day before.[67] Had Grouchy pushed forward to Moustier and Ottignies on the morning of the 18th, even nearly as quickly as he had fallen back from Wavre—nay, had he marched from Walhain to Waterloo at an equal rate of speed—he would have turned the scales of fortune in favour of the arms of France.

★★★★★★

Meantime Thielmann, deceived by Pajol—he masked the retreat with remarkable skill, and successfully rejoined the mass of the ar-

---

65. Thiers (*Histoire du Consulat et de l'Empire*, vi.) relates that Napoleon ordered Grouchy to retreat on Namur, but he gives no authority. Charras (2) asserts that Napoleon gave no such orders. H. Houssaye (*1815 Waterloo*) says the retreat, by Napoleon's directions, was to be either on Philippeville or on Givet. This seems probable.
66. Grouchy, too, had to carry his sick and wounded men with him in his retreat. This must have hampered him to some extent, and there was no such impediment on June 18.

my—had continued to fall back for some hours, and did not turn to pursue Grouchy until it was too late. Pirch, too, at the head of troops worn out by the harassing marches of two days, only reached Mellery by the night of the 19th, still some miles from the road from Nivelles to Namur; Thielmann was as yet far away and backward. Besides, the united forces of the Prussian chiefs were not superior to those of Grouchy in numbers; they were converging, at wide distances, against a concentrated enemy; their movements were necessarily, therefore, cautious; they had hardly a chance of defeating Grouchy.

On the 20th the French army resumed its movement, but this was imperilled for a time by an untoward accident. Grouchy, in command of the corps of Gérard, and encumbered by the charge of many sick and wounded men, had ordered Vandamme to cover the retreat; but Vandamme, always a bad companion in arms, had left his troops and gone off to Namur, conduct for which no kind of excuse can be made; his corps was attacked by Thielmann's horsemen on the morning of the 20th, and for a time was in some danger. Simultaneously the advanced guard of Pirch, moving from Mellery, had approached Grouchy; but the Marshal, a really good cavalry officer, succeeded in baffling Thielmann's efforts. Vandamme, hastening back from Namur, kept the enemy at bay; Grouchy and the men of Gérard reached the town in safety; Vandamme followed at a short distance.

The population of Namur detested the Prussians, and felt generous sympathies with the French in their distress. They gave Grouchy every assistance in their power; his army before long was across the Sambre. Teste, another skilful and bold officer, repelled the attack made by the Prussians on the place, and beat them back with not an inconsiderable loss. Meanwhile Grouchy had continued his movement; his army, almost intact, had come under the guns of Givet by the evening of June 21.[67] The intelligence and the resource he had shown in the retreat would have saved Napoleon three days before.

---

67. For the retreat of Grouchy, see Grouchy, *Relation Succincte*; Ollech, 263-269; Wagner, iv.; Charras, 2; H. Houssaye, 1815 *Waterloo* 2, and *The Battle of Wavre and Grouchy's Retreat* by W. Hyde Kelly, published by Leonaur. Chesney, a detractor of Napoleon, and an apologist of Grouchy (*Waterloo Lectures*), extols the retreat as a grand operation of war. It really was a well-combined movement of a very ordinary kind. Thielmann lost fifteen hours; Pirch's troops were unable to press a pursuit; and, besides, Thielmann and Pirch had not the means of overpowering or intercepting Grouchy. What is striking in the retreat was the celerity of the march, the very opposite of the hesitations, the delays, and the negligence of June 17 and 18. This makes Grouchy's conduct all the more inexcusable.

★★★★★★

By the last days of June Grouchy, who had been made the commander of all the military forces which had invaded Belgium, had brought his own corps and the remains of the Waterloo army with little loss under the walls of Paris; a considerable number of troops were within the city, and Paris was in a good state of defence along its northern front. At this moment the Prussian army, diminished by the corps of Pirch detached in the rear, and now not more than 60,000 strong, was around Gonesse, a few miles from the capital; the army of Wellington was near Gournay, at least two marches distant. This separation of the hostile forces gave an opportunity to Napoleon's genius. From his retreat at Malmaison he proposed to fall on Blucher with 70,000 or 80,000 men, who could have been assembled; he pledged himself to gain a signal victory; he promised that when this had been won he would instantly lay down his command.

Napoleon to Grouchy.

(*June* 16.)

Au Maréchal Comte Grouchy, Commandant l'Aile Droite de l'Armée du Nord.

CHARLEROI,
16 *juin*, 1815.

MON COUSIN,

Je vous envoie Labédoyère, mon aide de camp, pour vous porter la présente lettre. Le major-général a dû vous faire connaître mes intentions; mais, comme il a des officiers mal montés, mon aide de camp arrivera peut-être avant. Mon intention est que, comme commandant l'aile droite, vous preniez le commandement du 3e corps que commande le Général Vandamme, du 4e corps que commande le Général Gérard, des corps de cavalerie que commandent les Généraux Pajol, Milhaud, et Exelmans; ce qui ne doit pas faire loin de 50,000 hommes. Rendez vous avec cette aile droite à Sombreffe. Faites partir en conséquence, de suite, les corps des Généraux Pajol, Milhaud, Exelmans, et Vandamme, et sans vous arrêter, continuez votre mouvement sur Sombreffe. Le 4e corps, qui est à Châtelet, reçoit directement l'ordre de se rendre à Sombreffe sans passer pas Fleurus. Cette observation est importante, parce que je porte mon quartier-général à Fleurus et qu'il faut éviter les encombrements. Envoyez de suite un officier au Général Gérard pour lui faire connaître votre mouvement, et qu'il exécute le sien de suite.

Mon intention est que tous les généraux prennent directement vos ordres; ils ne prendront les miens que lorsque je serai présent. Je serai entre dix et onze heures à Fleurus: je me rendrai à Sombreffe laissant ma Garde, infanterie et cavalerie, à Fleurus; je ne la conduirais à Sombreffe qu'en cas qu'elle fût nécessaire. Si l'ennemi est à Sombreffe, je veux l'attaquer; je veux même l'attaquer à Gembloux et m'emparer aussi de cette position, mon intention étant après avoir connu ces deux positions, de partir cette nuit, et d'opérer avec mon aile gauche, que commande le Maréchal Ney, sur les Anglais. Ne perdez donc point un moment, parce que plus vite je prendrai mon parti, mieux cela vaudra pour la suite de mes opérations. Je suppose que vous êtes à Fleurus.

Communiquez constamment avec le Général Gérard, afin qu'il puisse vous aider pour attaquer Sombreffe, s'il était nécessaire. La division Girard est à portée de Fleurus ; n'en disposez point à moins de necessité absolue, parce qu'elle doit marcher toute la nuit. Laissez aussi ma jeune Garde et toute son artillerie à Fleurus.

Le Comte de Valmy, avec ses deux divisions de cuirassiers, marche sur la route de Bruxelles : il se lie avec le Maréchal Ney, pour contribuer à l'opération de ce soir, à l'aile gauche.

Comme je vous l'ai dit, je serai de dix à onze heures à Fleurus. Envoyez-moi des rapports sur tout ce que vous apprendrez. Veillez à ce que la route de Fleurus soit libre. Toutes les données que j'ai sont que les Prussiens ne peuvent point nous opposer plus de 40,000 hommes.

NAPOLÉON.*

SOULT TO GROUCHY.
(June 16.)

Au Maréchal Grouchy.

MONSIEUR LE MARÉCHAL,

L'Empereur ordonne que vous vous mettiez en marche avec les 1er, 2e et 4e corps de cavalerie et que vous les dirigiez sur Sombreffe, où vous prendrez position. Je donne pareil ordre à Monsieur le Lieutenant-Général Vandamme pour le 3e corps d'infanterie, et à Monsieur le Lieutenant-Général Gérard pour le 4e corps, et je préviens ces deux généraux qu'ils sont sous vos ordres, et qu'ils doivent vous envoyer immédiatement des officiers pour vous instruire de leur marche et prendre des instructions. Je leur dis cependant que lorsque Sa Majesté sera présente, ils pourront recevoir d'elle des ordres directs, et qu'ils devront continuer de m'envoyer des rapports de service et les états qu'ils ont l'habitude de me fournir.

Je préviens aussi Monsieur le Général Gérard que dans ses mouvements sur Sombreffe il doit laisser la ville de Fleurus à gauche, afin d'éviter l'encombrement. Ainsi, vous lui donnerez une direction pour qu'il marche, d'ailleurs bien réuni, à portée du 3e corps, et soit en mesure de concourir à l'attaque de Sombreffe, si l'ennemi fait résistance.

Vous donnerez aussi des instructions en conséquence à

Monsieur le Lieutenant-Général Comte Vandamme.

J'ai l'honneur de vous prévenir que Monsieur le Comte de Valmy a réçu ordre de se rendre à Gosselies, où, avec le 3e corps de cavalerie, il sera à la disposition de Monsieur le Prince de Moskova.

Le 1er régiment de hussards rentrera au 1er corps de cavalerie dans la journée. Je prendrai à ce sujet les ordres de l'Empereur. J'ai l'honneur de vous prévenir que Monsieur le Maréchal Prince de la Moskova reçoit ordre de se porter avec le 1er et le 2e corps d'infanterie et le 3e de cavalerie à l'intersection des chemins dits des Trois-Bras, sur la route de Bruxelles, et qu'il détachera un fort corps à Marbais pour se lier avec vous sur Sombreffe et seconder au besoin vos opérations.

Aussitôt que vous vous serez rendu maître de Sombreffe, il faudra envoyer une avant-garde à Gembloux, et faire reconnaître toutes les directions qui aboutissent à Sombreffe, particulièrement la grande route de Namur, en même temps que vous établirez vos communications avec Monsieur le Maréchal Ney.

La Garde Impériale se dirige sur Fleurus.

      Le Maréchal Duc de Dalmatie.*

Napoleon to Grouchy.

(June 17.)

Monsieur le Maréchal,

  Rendez vous à Gembloux avec le corps de cavalerie du Général Pajol, la cavalerie légère du 4e corps, et le corps de cavalerie du Général Exelmans, la division du Général Teste dont vous aurez un soin particulier, étant détachée de son corps d'armée, et les 3e et 4e corps d'infanterie. Vous vous ferez éclairer sur la direction de Namur et de Maëstricht, et vous poursuivrez l'ennemi. Éclairez sa marche et instruisez-moi de ses mouvements, de manière que je puisse pénétrer ce qu'il veut faire. Je porte mon quartier général aux Quatre-Chemins, où ce matin étaient encore les Anglais. Notre communication sera donc directe par la route pavée de Namur. Si l'ennemi a évacué Namur, écrivez au général commandant la deuxième division militaire, à Charlemont, de faire occuper Namur par quelques bataillons de garde nationale et quelques batteries de canon qu'il formera à Charlemont. Il donnera ce commandement à un maréchal de camp.

Il est important de pénétrer ce que l'ennemi veut faire : ou il se sépare des Anglais, ou ils veulent se réunir encore pour couvrir Bruxelles et Liége, en tentant le sort d'une nouvelle bataille. Dans tous les cas, tenez constamment vos deux corps d'infanterie réunis dans une lieue de terrain, et occupez tous les soirs une bonne position militaire, ayant plusieurs débouchés de retraite. Placez des détachements de cavalerie intermédiaire, pour communiquer avec le quartier général.

Dicté par l'Empereur, en l'absence du Major-Général.

Le Grand Maréchal Bertrand.*

Grouchy to Napoleon.
(*Written at 10 p.m. on June 17.*)

Sire,

J'ai l'honneur de vous rendre compte que j'occupe Gembloux et que ma cavalerie est à Sauvenière. L'ennemi fort d'environ trente-cinq mille hommes continue son mouvement de retraite ; on lui a saisi ici un parc de quatre cents bêtes à cornes, des magasins et des bagages.

Il paraît, d'après tous les rapports, qu'arrivés à Sauvenière, les Prussiens se sont divisés en deux colonnes ; l'une a dû prendre la route de Wavre en passant par Sart-les-Walhain ; l'autre colonne paraît s'être dirigée sur Perwez.

On peut peut-être en inférer qu'une portion va joindre Wellington, et que le centre, qui est l'armée de Blücher, se retire sur Liége ; une autre colonne avec de l'artillerie ayant fait son mouvement de retraite par Namur, le Général Exelmans a ordre de pousser, ce soir, six escadrons, sur Sart-les-Walhain, et trois escadrons sur Perwez. *D'après leur rapport, si la masse des Prussiens se retire sur Wavre, je la suivrai dans cette direction, afin qu'ils ne puissent pas gagner Bruxelles, et de les séparer de Wellington.* Si, au contraire, mes renseignements prouvent que la principale force prussienne a marché sur Perwez, je me dirigerai par cette ville à la poursuite de l'ennemi.

Les Généraux Thielmann et Borstell faisaient partie de l'armée que Votre Majesté a battue hier ; ils étaient encore ce matin à dix heures ici, et ont annoncé que vingt mille hommes des leurs avaient été mis hors de combat. Ils ont demandé en partant les distances de Wavre, Perwez et Hannut. Blücher a été blessé légèrement au bras, ce qui ne l'a pas empêché de continuer à commander après s'être fait panser.

Il n'a point passé par Gembloux.

Je suis avec respect,
Sire,
de Votre Majesté
le fidèle sujet,
Signé : Le Maréchal Comte De Grouchy.*

Particulars Regarding Marshal Grouchy's Army
By Sir John Sinclair Bart

I was fortunate enough to meet at Brussels with some of the most distinguished officers who had served in Grouchy's army; and with great readiness they answered the several questions I put to them, regarding that part of the French force. I shall here give a translation of the questions sent and the answers they returned, which contain some interesting particulars.

1. At what time was the corps of Marshal Grouchy separated from the grand army?

Answer. On the morning of the 17th of June.

2. What was its force, and the generals by whom it was commanded?

Answer. The force consisted in all of 45,000 men; of whom 39,000 were infantry, and 6000 cavalry. The principal officers were Generals Vandamme, Gerard, and Excelmans.

3. What were the orders given to the marshal, and what progress did he make in their execution?

Answer. The orders of the marshal were to march upon the army of the enemy, so as to prevent the junction between Wellington and Blucher. He arrived to carry that object into effect at Gembloux on the 17th, which the Prussian army had quitted about twelve at noon for Wavre. The marshal left Gembloux with his army on the morning of the 18th, to find out the Prussians, and to fight them. The second corps of cavalry, consisting of 4000 men, commanded by General Excelmans, discovered the rearguard of the Prussians near a place called Baraque, about ten o'clock in the morning. General Excelmans brought his cavalry to the Dyle, ready to pass that river, when about twelve the marshal arrived, with General Vandamme's corps, and gave orders to march upon Wavre; this they did, after we had defeated the rearguard of the Prussian army, which were from eight to ten thousand men.

4. Did you hear at Wavre the firing at the Battle of Waterloo, or Mount St. Jean?

Answer. About mid-day the cannonade was heard, and it was then that General Gerard, and several other officers, insisted strongly with the marshal to cross the Dyle, and to approach nearer to the emperor, leaving a small corps of observation before the Prussians, who had been beat, and had retired to Wavre. But the marshal constantly refused, and continued his route on Wavre. General Excelmans commanded the advanced guard, and would not have quitted the Dyle, had it not been in consequence of express orders given by the marshal in person, which he was compelled to obey.

5. To what circumstance was it owing that the army of Marshal Grouchy was of no use at the Battle of Waterloo, or Mount St. Jean?

Answer. Because the marshal committed the fault of employing his whole army, whereas at the utmost, 10,000 men would have been sufficient to have kept the rearguard of the Prussians in check.

6. Did Napoleon send any orders to Marshal Grouchy during the battle?

Answer. Several officers were sent before mid-day by the emperor to search for Marshal Grouchy, but only one of them (Colonel Zenowitz) arrived at Wavre, and not till about six o'clock in the evening. The marshal then resolved to pass the Dyle at Limale, with a part of his army; but it was then too late.

7. What became afterwards of General Grouchy's army?

Answer. It was about eleven o'clock in the morning of the 19th, that the marshal learnt that the emperor had been beaten. The attack which he intended to make on the road from Brussels to Louvain was therefore given up, and the army passed the Dyle at four points—Wavre, Limale, Limilet and Ottigny. General Excelmans with his corps pushed on to Namur, where he arrived in the evening, and where the marshal arrived next day. The allies attacked the rearguard, commanded by Vandamme. The conflict was very obstinate, but the allies suffered so much that our retreat afterwards was unmolested.

These officers added, that in their opinion, "*Si les ordres de l'Empereur eussent etes executes, par le Marechal Grouchy, les armees Anglaise et Prussienne etoient perdues sans resource.*" This cannot be admitted. It is said that Grouchy was over-persuaded by Vandamme to push on to Wavre, in the hopes of getting first to Brussels, and securing the plunder of that town to themselves.

General Vandamme

Extract of a Letter from Marshal Ney to the Duke of Otranto, June 26, 1825

.....On the 17th the army marched in the direction of Mount St. Jean. On the 18th the battle commenced at one o'clock, and, though the bulletin which gives an account of it does not mention my name, I believe that I have occasion to affirm that I was present. Lieutenant-General Comte Drouet has already spoken of this battle in the Chamber of Peers, and his relation is correct, with the exception, however, of some important facts, which he either suppressed or knew not, but which it is my duty to disclose.

About seven in the evening, after the most dreadful carnage I ever witnessed, General Labedoyere came to inform me, on the part of the Emperor, that Marshal Grouchy had arrived on our right, and was attacking the left of the united English and Prussians. The General in passing through the lines, circulated this news among the soldiers, whose courage and devotedness remained unaltered, and who were giving fresh proofs of it at that moment, notwithstanding the fatigue with which they were exhausted. But what was my astonishment, I ought to say indignation, when I learned a few moments afterwards, that not only Marshal Grouchy had not arrived to our support, as the whole army had been taught to believe, but that between 40,000 and 50,000 Prussians were attacking our extreme right, and forcing it to fall back.

Either the Emperor had deceived himself as to the time in which Marshal Grouchy could have been able to support him, or the march of the Marshal had been more retarded by the efforts of the enemy than had been calculated upon. The fact is, that, at the moment when the arrival was announced to us, he was still only in the neighbourhood of Wavres on the Dyle; which, with regard to us, was the same as if he had been a hundred leagues from the place of battle.

Soon after I observed the arrival of four regiments of the middle-guard, led by the Emperor in person, who wished to renew the attack with these troops, in order to penetrate the enemy's centre. He ordered me to march at their head with General Friant. Generals, officers, soldiers, all displayed the greatest intrepidity. But the corps was too weak to resist for any length of time the forces which were employed to oppose it, and we had soon to renounce the hope which this attack for a few moments afforded. General Friant was struck by a ball at my side. I had a horse killed and was thrown down under him. The brave men who survived this battle will, I trust, do me the justice to state, that they saw me fighting foot to foot, sword in hand, and I was one of the last who left the scene of carnage, at the moment when obliged to retreat.

Meanwhile the Prussians continued their offensive movement, and our right was sensibly giving way; the English in their turn advanced. There yet remained to us four squares of old guard placed advantageously for the retreat; these brave grenadiers, the elite of the army who were forced to fall back successively, only yielded the ground foot by foot, until, finally overpowered by numbers, they were almost completely destroyed. From that time the retrograde movement was most decided, and the army formed only a confused column; there was however then no shouting, nor cry of *suave qui peut*, as has been calumniously imputed to the army in the Bulletin. For myself, being continually in the rearguard, which I followed on foot, having had all my horses killed, worn out with fatigue, covered with contusions, and having no longer any strength to walk, I owe my life to a corporal of the guard, who supported me in the march, and never abandoned me in this retreat.

About eleven at night I fell in with Lieutenant-General Lefebvre Desnouettes; and one of his officers, Major Schmidt, had the generosity to give me the only horse which remained to him. Thus I arrived at Marchiennes-au-pont, at four in the morning, alone, without officers, ignorant of the fate of the Emperor, whom sometime before the termination of the battle, I had entirely lost sight of, and whom I supposed to be killed or taken.

General P. Lacroix, chief of the staff of the second corps, whom I found in this city, having told me that the Emperor was at Charleroi,

I supposed that His Majesty intended to place himself at the head of Marshal Grouchy's corps, in order to cover the Sambre, and to facilitate to the troops the means of rallying near Avesnes, and in this persuasion I proceeded to Beaumont, but parties of cavalry having followed us very closely, and intercepted the roads to Maubeuge and Philippeville, I found it impossible to stop a single soldier at this point, so as to oppose the progress of a victorious enemy. I continued my journey to Avesnes, where I could obtain no information concerning the enemy.....

Marshal Ney

General Gaspard Gourgard

Extract from Remarks on General Gourgaud's Account of the Campaign of 1815
(*Blackwood's Magazine*)

Besides this sweeping charge, that the French Generals under Bonaparte did not in this campaign do their utmost to enforce and carry through his plans, distinct errors are imputed to one or two of them by name. Upon the 15th July, Vandamme, it is said, arrived at Charleroi four hours later than he ought to have done, which is described as "*un funeste contretemps.*"—Again, upon the juncture of the corps of Vandamme with that of Grouchy at Gilly, it is stated, that these generals, deceived by false intelligence, remained stationary, instead of attacking a small part of the Prussian army under Zeithen, which they had mistaken for Blucher's main body. And Grouchy is elsewhere censured (with more apparent reason), for not moving to his left, and placing himself in communication with Bonaparte, instead of remaining with his division at Wavre during the whole of the 18th.

These and other charges against Vandamme and Grouchy, are made with moderation, and, under qualifying circumstances of excuse and of commendation. Upon two individuals, the unmitigated censure of Gourgaud, and of we suppose, Bonaparte, descends in full stream. Joachim Murat and Michael Ney. By a singular coincidence they are both *no more*—the safer subjects, therefore, to be converted into convenient scapegoats. The dead can neither vindicate themselves, nor retort upon others; and the blame which if imputed to *them*, Grouchy or Vandamme might have flung back in the face of their censor, may be securely piled on the bloody graves of Ney and Murat.

The Combats of Wavre and the Retreat of Grouchy
(Extract from *1815, Waterloo* by Henry Houssaye)

1

We have seen that, on June 18th, about noon, Marshal Grouchy, in the course of his discussion with Gérard at Walhain, had received an *aide-de-camp* from Exelmans, who informed him of the Prussian rear guard before Wavre.

Between nine and ten o'clock Exelmans' two divisions of dragoons had arrived at La Baraque, at five kilometres from that little town. Some scouts who had pushed beyond the defile of La Huzelle reported a body of Prussian troops, consisting of cavalry, infantry, and artillery, in position upon the heights of Wavre. It was the entire corps of Pirch, still on the right bank of the Dyle, and two cavalry regiments of the *landwehr*, composing the rear guard of Bülow. Although he had orders to pursue the enemy closely, Exelmans feared to engage these masses with only his cavalry in a region so wooded. He knew, moreover, from new information or indications, that the Prussian Army would manoeuvre to join the English. He thought that Grouchy would interrupt the march on Wavre, henceforth without object, in order to pass the Dyle at the nearest point.

With the design of preparing for this movement, he directed towards that river the brigade of Vincent; it took position at the farm of La Plaquerie, at the distance of a cannon-shot from Ottignies. Exelmans sent towards Neuf Sart the brigade of Berton to reconnoitre the right, left at La Baraque an advance guard of two squadrons, and fell back with the bulk of the division of Chastel nearly a league in the rear, near Corbaix. It was during this halt that he sent an *aide-de-camp* to Grouchy to inform him of the presence of the Prussians before

Wavre and of the dispositions that he had made.

The corps of Vandamme was then halted at Nil Saint-Vincent, in conformity with the orders of Grouchy of the day before. On the evening of June 17th, the Marshal, in spite of all his information concerning the march of the Prussians towards Wavre, was still so undecided touching the direction to take that he had directed Vandamme to advance only as far as Walhain. A little later, about eleven or twelve at night, he had written to him as follows:

"I have forgotten to tell you to push beyond Walhain, in order that General Gérard may take position in the rear. I think we will go farther than Walhain; it will then be rather a halt than a definite position."

On the morning of the 18th, on breaking camp, Grouchy, fully decided from that time to march on Wavre, would have had plenty of time to rectify these instructions and to order Vandamme to follow as rapidly as possible the cavalry of Exelmans. He did not think of this. Vandamme, after having passed Walhain, halted at Nil Saint-Vincent, pending new orders.

About one o'clock. Grouchy warned by Exelmans' *aide-de-camp*, Commandant d'Estourmel, that the Prussian rear guard was in sight, arrived at Nil Saint-Vincent. He gave to Vandamme and sent to Exelmans the order to put the troops on the march. A little before two o'clock, as the advance of the dragoons approached La Baraque, the two squadrons that had been left there as an advance guard were attacked by the 10th Prussian Hussars, debouching on their left flank. This regiment, with two battalions and two guns, formed the detachment of Colonel Ledebur, posted in observation at Mont Saint-Guilbert.

Until one o'clock Ledebur had not budged. Badly informed by his patrols and *videttes*, he was completely ignorant of the approach of the French Army, as well as the *pointe* pushed in the morning to La Baraque by the two divisions of Exelmans, and the occupation of the farm of La Plaquerie by the brigade of Vincent. Although surrounded by enemies, he did not know it. Warned, finally, of the presence of the French at Nil Saint Vincent and on the route of Wavre, Ledebur saw that his direct line of retreat was in danger of being intercepted. He pushed rapidly his hussars through the fields to La Baraque, whilst his two battalions gained at a run, by way of Bruyères and Bloc-Ry, the wood of La Huzelle, which bordered the road on both sides, to the north of La Baraque, and made of it a kind of defile.

The hussars drove back the two French squadrons to the east of the road, kept up for some minutes the combat, and then, on the approach of the bulk of the dragoons, they withdrew through the defile, which had just been occupied by the sharpshooters of Ledebur. Infantry was required to dislodge the latter. The dragoons made way for the head of Vandamme's column; it attacked without delay. Two battalions of Brause's division, which were still with Langen's division (both belonging to Pirch's corps), on the right bank of the Dyle, had been sent to the support of Ledebur.

The defence was obstinate. Grouchy, unknown to Exelmans, had recalled from the banks of the Dyle the brigade of Vincent, All the dragoons were assembled. He ordered Exelmans to turn the position towards Dion-le-Mont with these three thousand horsemen. The manoeuvre, well conceived, but effected too late or two slowly, did not give the expected results. Before the French cavalry had finished its movement, the Prussians had fallen back on Wavre. Vandamme passed the defile. He had orders from Grouchy to pursue the enemy even upon the heights which dominate this town, and to take position there pending new instructions.

In spite of the assurance with which .he had spoken to Gérard, Grouchy was none the less troubled by the cannonade heard on his left. He advanced at a gallop towards Limelette, "in order," says he, "to form a better opinion as to the causes of this cannonade." He finally acquired the conviction that a great battle was being waged upon the edge of the Forest of Soignes. On regaining the route of Wavre, between half-past three and four o'clock, he received the Emperor's (or rather Soult's) letter, written from Caillou, at ten in the morning. It was addressed to "*Marshal Grouchy, at Gembloux, or somewhere in front of this town.*"

The courier, Adjutant-Commandant Zenowicz, had been forced to pass through Genappe, Sombreffe, and Gembloux. This made a journey of ten leagues. Zenowicz, however, might have effected it in less time than it took him to do so. Besides, had this despatch, which directed Grouchy to march on Wavre while connecting the communications with the Imperial Army, reached him sooner, it would have led to no change in his essential dispositions.

After having read it, he even remarked to his *aide-de-camp* Bella "that he congratulated himself on having so well carried out the Emperor's instructions in marching on Wavre, instead of listening to the advice of General Gérard"; and he replied to Berthezène, who had sent one of his *aides-de-camp* to inform him of the march of the Prussian columns in the direction of the fire: "Let the General be tranquil; we are on the right road. I have just heard from the Emperor, and he orders me to march on Wavre."

The Emperor also ordered him, as subsidiary, it is true, to connect the communications with the main body of the Army. Grouchy took some tardy measures to execute these instructions. Pajol had just informed him, through an *aide-de-camp*, that the right column, in its march from Grand Leez to Tourinnes, had discovered no trace of the enemy. Grouchy sent back the *aide-de-camp* with the order for Pajol to advance immediately with the 2nd Cavalry Corps and the division of Teste to Limale and to pass the Dyle by main force. Grouchy was ignorant of the value of time, otherwise he would have selected to capture the bridge of Limale, not Pajol, who, at Tourinnes, was distant three leagues and a half from it; but the cavalry of General Vallin, which was a league from the Dyle, and the division of Hulot, of the corps of Gérard, which had arrived at La Baraque;

The despatch sent to Pajol, Grouchy galloped towards Wavre, against which he intended to direct the attack in person. The impetuous Vandamme had not waited for him. Despite the orders of the Marshal, without reconnoitring the position, and without preparing the way with his artillery, he had launched *à la française* the entire division of Habert against the town in columns of assault.

The second *echelon* of the corps of Ziethen (divisions of Brause and Langen and the cavalry of Sohr) had passed the Dyle after the combat at the defile of La Huzelle and had marched towards Chapelle Saint-Lambert. But there still remained to defend Wavre and its approaches almost all of the corps of Thielmann. Believing at first that the deployment of the cavalry of Exelmans between Sainte-Anne and Dion-le-Mont was only a demonstration, Thielmann had set his troops in motion in the direction of Couture Saint-Germain; two battalions alone were to remain to guard Wavre.

Then, at sight of Vandamme, who debouched in front of the town, he had caused the positions which he had just evacuated to be reoccupied. The divisions of Kempher and Luck, three battalions of the division of Borcke and the cavalry of Hobe, established themselves in Wavre, Basse-Wavre, and upon the heights of the left bank, of the Dyle. The division of Stulpnagel came to occupy Bierges; the detachment from the corps of Ziethen (three battalions and three squadrons, under Von Stengel), detached to guard the bridge of Limale, was maintained at that post.

The infantry of Habert quickly dislodged the Prussians from the *faubourg* of Wavre; but their furious charge was arrested at the Dyle, which separated the town from the *faubourg*. The two bridges were strongly barricaded and enfiladed by batteries established upon the different heights in the inclined streets abutting on the river; finally, more than a thousand sharpshooters were concealed in the houses of the left bank. General Habert, Colonel Dubalen, of the 64th, and 600 men were put *hors de combat* in a few minutes. Powerless to carry the bridge, the soldiers hesitated to retire, for fear of being exposed to the terrible fire of the Prussian batteries, which swept the approaches of the faubourg and the steep acclivities of the right bank. They sheltered themselves in the streets parallel with the Dyle. "They were engulfed," says Grouchy, "in a kind of *cul-de-sac*."

2

After having examined attentively the position, Grouchy resolved to second the attack on Wavre by two other attacks above and below the town. Some reinforcements entered the faubourg; one of Lefol's battalions was detached to pass the Dyle at the mill bridge of Bierges; and Exelmans advanced with his dragoons in front of Basse-Wavre. As the Marshal finished taking these dispositions, he received, about five o'clock, the dispatch which Soult had sent him from the battlefield at half-past one, and which terminated as follows:

> At this moment the battle is engaged along the line of Waterloo in front of the Forest of Soignes. So you will manoeuvre to join our right. We believe that we see now the corps of Bülow upon the heights of Saint-Lambert. So you will not lose an instant in approaching and joining us, in order that you may crush Bülow, whom you will take in the very act.

The despatch, written with a pencil, was partly effaced, and almost illegible. Grouchy and many officers of his staff read this letter as follows:

"*La battaile est gagnée*" ("The battle is gained"), instead of "*La battaile est engage*" ("Battle is engaged").

They wished to interrogate the courier. But Grouchy pretends that this officer was too drunk to answer. At any rate, the Marshal had only to reflect. It was evident that a despatch written at one o'clock could not call gained an action which the noise of the cannon, more and more violent, indicated only too well still lasted at five.

However, whether the battle was engaged or gained, the order of the Emperor existed none the less, formal and imperative: it was necessary to march on Saint-Lambert in order to crush Bülow. Grouchy understood it; but he displayed neither resolution nor method in his dispositions. Two of Vandamme's divisions were sufficient to occupy the Prussians before Wavre. It seems then that the Marshal ought to have directed immediately towards Limale Vandamme's third division as well as Exelmans' eight regiments of dragoons, whose diversion upon Basse-Wavre was no longer useful.

But Grouchy, by the strangest of strategical conceptions, wished at the same time to capture Wavre with half of his army and to direct the other half on Saint-Lambert by the bridge of Limale. He left then before the Prussian positions all of the 3rd Corps and Exelmans' cavalry, and sent his *aide-de-camp* Pont-Bellanger to carry the verbal order to Pajol, who had left Tourinnes, to hasten his march on Limale. "Never has the Emperor been so great!" said Pont-Bellanger, on approaching Pajol. "The battle is gained, and only the cavalry is awaited to finish the rout."

At the same time that he despatched this order to Pajol, Grouchy came at a gallop with Gérard to La Baraque to direct from thence on Limale the 4th Corps, whose leading division (General Hulot) had alone arrived upon the heights of Wavre. Is it true, as Grouchy says, that the other two divisions of the 4th Corps (Vichery and Pécheux) had not yet attained La Baraque at six in the evening; that, tired of waiting for them, the Marshal returned in front of Wavre, leaving the order for these two divisions to march directly on Limale; finally, that, this order having been badly interpreted, Vichery and Pécheux continued their movement on Wavre?

Or should we rather believe that Grouchy found these divisions at La Baraque; that he gave them the order to march on Limale, but that the head of column got lost *en route* for want of a guide, and resumed its march towards Wavre? It appears impossible to get at the truth in the midst of the contradictory testimonies of Gérard, General Hulot, and of Grouchy himself, whose own assertions do not agree with each other. It is certain, however, that Grouchy went to La Baraque and then returned to Wavre.

The combat continued to rage fiercely on both sides of the Dyle. The attack on the bridge of Bierges by the battalion of Lefol had been repulsed. Grouchy, bent on passing the Dyle at this point, ordered Gérard to renew the attack with a battalion of Hulot's division. Gérard having remarked to him that it would be better to cause the detachment of Lefol to be supported by other troops of the same corps, he received badly this very apposite observation. Gérard then transmitted the order to Hulot, who conducted in person to the assault a battalion of the 9th Light. To reach the bridge, it had to cross some very marshy ground intersected parallel with the Dyle by ditches, very deep and wide.

Hulot directed the men to throw themselves into these ditches, if they could not leap them. They found themselves in water from four to six feet in depth, and the skirmishers were on the point of being drowned; the assistance of their comrades was necessary to extricate them from their dangerous position. During this time the bullets fell as thick as hail. Rebuffed, the soldiers fell back. Grouchy and Gérard, the latter at the head of another battalion, arrived about this time on the edge of the meadow. Gérard, little accustomed to spare himself, exposed himself all the more, as he had reasons to be in a very bad humour. He was shot through the body and carried to the rear. Grouchy then ordered General Baltus, commanding the artillery, to replace Gérard at the head of the assaulting column.

The latter having positively refused to do so, Grouchy leaped from his horse, crying: "If one can no longer command the obedience of his subordinates, he should at least know how to die." This third assault failed, like the preceding ones. Grouchy left the division of Hulot before Bierges, as if he had wished, says Hulot, to make new dispositions for attacking the mill; then, suddenly changing his mind, he rejoined the other two divisions of Gérard and advanced with them towards Limale.

During these vain assaults, one continued to skirmish in front of Basse-Wavre, and at Wavre the fight was pursued with terrible ferocity. Vandamme made as many as thirteen attacks without being able to wrest from the Prussians this little town, which had been transformed into a veritable fortress. At eleven in the evening the combat still raged.

When Marshal Grouchy arrived at Limale, at nightfall, the bridge over the Dyle was free. Renewing the audacious manoeuvre of the preceding year at Montereau, Pajol had launched at full speed the hussars of General Vallin upon this bridge, which, however, was accessible to only four horses arriving abreast, and which was defended by an entire battalion. The Prussians overthrown and sabred, the infantry of Teste and the rest of the cavalry passed the bridge behind the hussars and took position on the left bank. Von Stengel yielded Limale after a combat of some duration, and took up a position on the height which dominates this village.

In spite of the gathering darkness, the assault was vigorously conducted by Teste, when Grouchy debouched by the bridge of Limale with the divisions of Vichery and Pécheux. These reinforcements were necessary, for Thielmann, hearing the cannonade, had sent to the support of Stengel, by the left bank of the Dyle, the division of Stulpnagel and the cavalry of Hobe. The combat continued until eleven in the evening for the possession of the crest of the plateau, which, finally, remained in possession of the French. The road to Mont Saint-Jean was open: but for a long time the cannon of the Emperor had been silent.

3

The French bivouacked in squares, almost intermingled with the enemy, who occupied the wood of Rixensart. The advance posts were so close to each other that the bullets exchanged throughout the night fell in the rear of the first lines. At half-past eleven in the evening Grouchy wrote to Vandamme to rejoin him at once at Limale with the 3rd Corps. He intended to recommence the combat early in the morning, in order to join the Imperial Army at Brussels, for the report was circulated—we know not upon what grounds—that the Emperor had defeated the English.

The Prussian Staff was better informed. An officer of Marwitz's cavalry, sent on a reconnaissance, had reported that the French Army was in flight. Thenceforth reassured, Thielmann directed most of his troops upon the plateau of Limale, in order to resume the offensive at dawn. At three in the morning the cavalry of Hobe debouched from the wood of Rixensart with two horse batteries, which, in a few minutes, riddled with balls the French bivouacs. Grouchy, hastening upon the firing-line, ordered his batteries to reply; then, having formed all his force in line of battle, the cavalry of Pajol on the extreme left, the divisions of Pécheux and Vichery in the centre and in reserve, and the division of Teste on the right, he marched against the enemy.

After a stubborn defence, the Prussians yielded the wood of Rixensart. It was nearly eight o'clock. Thielmann received from Pirch positive information of the defeat of the French. The despatch added that the 2nd Corps was about to manoeuvre to intercept the retreat of Marshal Grouchy. The news of this great victory, which was immediately announced to the troops, reanimated them. Thielmann, pivoting upon his left wing, which still occupied the wood of Bierges, executed a change of front. By this movement the Prussian right found itself deployed parallel with the route from Wavre to Brussels.

The combat was resumed, not without advantage for the Prussians, till the division of Teste had carried the village and the mill of Bierges. In this assault General Penne, one of Teste's brigadiers, who was wounded himself, had his head carried away by a cannon-ball. Berthezène, posted on the right bank of the Dyle, had seconded the attack of Teste; the two divisions united. Thielmann, seeing his left outflanked and his right on the point of being turned by the cavalry of Pajol, which was manoeuvring towards Rosieren in order to get possession of the route of Brussels, put himself in retreat in the direction of Louvain.

The four battalions left in Wavre evacuated that position, and proceeded at first to La Bavette, from whence they were quickly dislodged by the advance guard of Vandamme. Notwithstanding the order of Grouchy to come to rejoin him at Limale with the 3rd Corps, Vandamme had remained all the morning before Wavre. He had only sent to the Marshal the dragoons of Exelmans and the division of Hulot, which he had caused to be relieved in front of Bierges by the division of Berthezène.

Master of the field of battle, upon which the Prussians had abandoned five pieces of artillery and numerous wounded, Grouchy had his right at La Bavette and his left beyond Rosieren. He was making his preparations to march on Brussels when, about half-past ten, an officer of the Major-General arrived. His haggard face, his eyes big with fright, and his enfeebled body appearing, like his horse, broken by fatigue, he seemed the living image of defeat.

Hardly able to collect his ideas and to find his speech, he related in so incoherent a manner the disaster of Mont Saint-Jean that the Marshal thought at first that he had an affair with a fool or a drunken man. To the questions asked him by Grouchy—if he was the bearer of an order; upon what point the retreat was to be effected; and if the Army had repassed the Sambre—the officer, instead of replying, recommenced the confused recital of the battle. Some precise details, seized in the midst of divagations, finally convinced Grouchy. It was not the moment to yield to grief; it was necessary to save what remained of the army.

Grouchy united his general officers in a sort of council of war. He announced to them the terrible news. While speaking he had, it has been said, tears in his eyes. The officers knew of the discussion that he had had the day before with Gérard at Walhain. The Marshal thought that the circumstances made it necessary for him to justify himself for not having listened to the counsel of his lieutenant.

"My honour," said he, "demands that I explain my dispositions of yesterday. The instructions which I had received from the Emperor forbade me to manoeuvre in any other direction than Wavre. I have been forced to reject the advice that Count Gérard believed he had a right to give me. I render justice to the talents and the brilliant valour of General Gérard; but, no doubt, you were as much astonished as myself that a general officer, ignorant of the Emperor's orders and of the information upon which the Marshal of France under whom he was placed acted, should permit himself to trace publicly for him his conduct.

"The advanced hour of the day, the distance at which we were from the point where the cannon was heard, and the state of the roads, rendered it impossible to arrive in time to take part in the action that was being fought. Besides, whatever may be the events that have taken place, the orders of the Emperor, of which I have just communicated to you the contents, did not permit of my acting otherwise than I have done."

After having pronounced these words, which were merely an apology for his conduct, the Marshal unfolded his plan of retreat. He had at first thought of advancing upon the rear of the Anglo-Prussians, in order to delay by this diversion their pursuit of the Imperial Army; but he quickly renounced this idea, whose sole result would have been the total destruction of his 30,000 men submerged, crushed by 150,000. For the same reason he wisely rejected the bold project of Vandamme, which consisted in marching on Brussels, where they would set free numerous prisoners, and in regaining the frontier towards Valenciennes or Lille by way of Enghien and Ath.

Vandamme supposed that on this side only a few detachments of the Allied Army would be encountered. Grouchy rightly preferred to take his line of retreat on Namur, Dinant, and Givet. It was necessary to make haste, for it was not only to be feared that the army would be harassed by Thielmann, who, no doubt, would resume the offensive at the first retrograde movement of the French, but that it would be attacked in flank by one of Blücher's army corps. Perhaps this detachment would even arrive in time to take position at Gembloux and bar the retreat.

This was, in fact, the object of the Prussians; and at eleven o'clock, when Grouchy still had his army beyond the Dyle, its front between Rosieren and La Bavette, Pirch, who had been detached from Rossomme in the night with the 2nd Corps, already occupied Mellery. He had nearly two hours the start of Grouchy, for the distance from Mellery to Gembloux is ten kilometres, as the crow flies, and from La Bavette to Gembloux, twenty.

The retreat began between eleven o'clock and noon. The dragoons of Exelmans, with the exception of the 20th Regiment placed under the orders of Vandamme, advanced very rapidly on Namur to seize the bridges over the Sambre; their advance guard reached there about four o'clock. The 4th Corps and the cavalry of Vallin repassed the Dyle at Limale and took the direct route to Gembloux; they bivouacked at night at two leagues beyond that village on the road leading from Nivelles to Namur, between Le Mazy and Temploux. Grouchy, who marched with this *echelon* of the army, established his headquarters in Temploux.

From La Bavette the corps of Vandamme withdrew to Wavre, remained in position there until late, and then marched by way of Dion-le-Mont, Tourinnes, and Grand Leez. It halted about eleven in the evening on the road from Gembloux to Namur, on a line with Temploux. Pajol, charged with forming the rear guard with the cavalry of General Soult and the indefatigable division of Teste, imposed on Thielmann by following him even near Saint-Achtenrode, where the latter took position. Then, when the entire corps of Vandamme had repassed the bridges of Wavre, Pajol put himself in retreat, gained Gembloux by way of Sauvenierre, and there established himself in bivouac in the night.

This hazardous retreat was not effected without some disorder; but not a shot was fired. Thielmann, whose corps was reduced to 12,500 men by the losses of the day before and of the morning, did not learn until very late of the retreat of the French. As to the 2nd Prussian Corps, though it had reached Mellery at noon, it had arrived there in the worst state of fatigue, for it had, so to speak, been on the march for twenty- four hours without intermission. Besides, it seems that Pirch did not feel strong enough to act alone. He was without news of Thielmann, whose cooperation he expected. He was unwilling or did not think it possible to lead further on this day his harassed soldiers.

4

The next day, June 20th, Pajol and Teste quitted Gembloux early in the morning, in accordance with the orders of Grouchy, and marched by way of Saint-Denis and Saint-Marc on Namur. About nine o'clock Grouchy likewise directed on Namur the 4th Corps, which convoyed all the wounded and the reserve park. The Marshal intended to traverse the town with this army corps, whilst that of Vandamme remained in position across the route of Gembloux until past noon to cover the movement.

But things did not pass exactly as the Marshal had planned. At the moment when the advance of the 4th Corps quitted Temploux a brisk cannonade was heard in front towards the left. Instead of bivouacking in the midst of his troops, Vandamme had gone to pass the night in Namur. He had not received the order, sent by Grouchy, to hold the position; and in the morning Generals Lefol, Berthezène, and Habert, left without instructions, had put themselves on the march for Namur and, by this movement, uncovered the flank of the 4th Corps. They were attacked near La Falise by more than thirty squadrons of Hobe, which Thielmann had caused to set out from Saint-Achtenrode at five in the morning with a horse battery, and which had made ten leagues in pursuit of the French.

At the same time Grouchy was informed that a considerable body of the enemy was debouching from Mazy. It was the advance guard of Pirch on the march from Mellery.

Grouchy found himself in grave peril, for if the infantry of Vandamme should withdraw too quickly beyond the Sambre, Hobe would bar to him the route of Namur while he was fighting Pirch. The troops, also understanding the danger, showed some uneasiness; the numerous wounded who had been brought from Limale and Wavre expressed by murmurs, groans, and cries of rage their fear of falling alive into the hands of the Prussians. Grouchy rode among the wagons with General Vichery. He said in a loud voice: "Be tranquil! We swear not to abandon you. But I am confident that our dispositions will save us."

Then, with the cavalry of General Vallin, he charged the Prussian squadrons which, having turned the divisions of Vandamme, flanked his line of retreat, and drove them back on the left. Continuing his march, he went to the support of Vandamme. In the meantime the 4th

Corps, which thenceforth found the road free, gained Namur with the wounded and the park; the rear guard, commanded by Vichery in person, arrested for some time at Boquet the Prussians of Pirch; it then withdrew, disputing the ground foot by foot.

Surprised by the sudden attack of the Prussian cavalry, the 3rd Corps found itself in a critical situation. A square of Lefol was broken; the men escaped the lances of the *Uhlans* only by seeking refuge in the woods. Two pieces of artillery were lost. The arrival of Grouchy arrested the enemy. The cavalry of Vallin charged at a gallop. Colonel Briqueville, who charged at the head of the 20th Dragoons, overthrew the furthest advanced of the Prussian squadrons, retook the two guns, and even captured a cannon. All of Hobe's cavalry fell back upon Pirch's corps, which debouched from Temploux.

On hearing the noise of the combat, Vandamme had hastened from Namur. Grouchy reiterated to him the order to cover the retreat of the 4th Corps. Vandamme re-formed his battalions, took position in front of the *faubourgs*, and succeeded in checking the Prussians. The cavalry, the 4th Corps, and the convoys entered Namur, where the Prussians were detested. The French brought with them the terrible hazards of war. They were none the less received as friends. The municipality distributed 100,000 rations of bread and the same number of brandy. The brave Namurois loaned their boats for the transportation of the wounded by the Meuse, and themselves aided in embarking them. The women brought, even under the cannon-balls of the enemy, food to the soldiers and assistance to the wounded.

The army passed through Namur without halting. First Grouchy, with the 4th Corps, and then Vandamme, wounded slightly, with the 3rd, passed the Sambre and plunged into the long defile formed by the Meuse and the Forest of Morlagne. The division of Teste was ordered to hold the town until night. To defend Namur, whose dilapidated fortifications were not proof against an escalade, Teste had eight field-pieces and 2,000 men at most. He distributed them upon the ramparts and at the three eastern gates—Louvain, Iron, and Saint-Nicholas.

Hardly were his men in position when Pirch launched his columns to the assault. Received by a discharge of grape and a rolling fire of musketry, the Prussians retreated, leaving upon the glacis a pile of dead and wounded. A second attack, in which Colonels Zastrow and Bismarck were mortally wounded, failed like the preceding. On account of the scarcity of cartridges, each Frenchman aimed carefully and brought down his Prussian. It was eight in the evening. Pirch, having lost 1,500 men, and despairing of capturing the place by main force, broke off the combat. But General Teste, almost out of ammunition, had already begun his retreat.

The Prussians, having discovered this, penetrated into the town through the windows and door of the custom-house, and pushed rapidly as far as the bridge of the Sambre. There, a detachment of engineers, posted in some houses which the sappers had had time to pierce with loopholes, checked them a long time by a sustained and well-aimed fire. This rear guard then withdrew by the gate of France, where a great quantity of fascines, bundles of straw, and pieces of wood soaked in tar had been accumulated. The sappers set fire to the pile. The gate and neighbouring houses burst into flames, closing the street to the Prussians.

During this combat the bulk of Grouchy's army had attained Dinant. On the next day, June 21st, all the army was assembled under the cannon of Givet.

If this march from Wavre to the frontier is not "one of the most astonishing retreats of modern military history," for the carelessness of Thielmann and the timidity of Pirch singularly facilitated it, it, nevertheless, does great honour to Grouchy. He did not despair when all hope seemed lost. He knew how to act with precision and rapidity. By the direction which he chose and by the dispositions which he took, he saved his army. We may ask ourselves, What would have happened if the unfortunate Marshal had shown on June 17th and 18th as much resolution, activity, military talent, and the same understanding of the exigencies of the situation?

Notes and Comments
(Extract from *The Battle of Wavre and Grouchy's Retreat,* by W. Hyde Kelly)

1.—The proportion of cavalry to infantry in Grouchy's force was large (more than one to five), but not excessive. He was given a task in which cavalry must play the chief part. At the close of such a battle as Ligny, the, infantry on both sides must be more or less exhausted, and it become the duty of the cavalry to pursue the retreating enemy. Cavalry alone, however, will effect little, if the enemy takes to rearguard positions; it must be supported or accompanied by artillery and infantry. It must be remembered that, of the two sides, the vanquished are the more exhausted, and the greater the enemy's anxiety to draw his troops clear of pursuit, the closer that pursuit must be. The French cavalry at Ligny, except Milhaud's *Cuirassiers*, had had little to do.

The proportion of cavalry to infantry in an army cannot be laid down by any hard-and-fast rule. Prince Kraft wrote after 1870:

> The duties of the cavalry are so comprehensive and so important, especially at the first moment of a war, that we cannot have too many cavalry ready for service.

But he was speaking of Germany. Continental armies require a far larger number of cavalry than our own; and not only for the reason that their other arms are so much more numerous than ours. The advance of modern armies is covered by a most numerous cavalry, sent out, as were the German cavalry in 1870, miles ahead, as a screen, and for the purpose of reconnaissance, or to harass the enemy's concentration and cut his communications.

2. *The French Corps* in 1815.—The French Corps in the 1815 Campaign were more independent than the Prussian Corps—that is to say, each corps, except Lobau's, was provided with, sufficient, cavalry and artillery to enable it. To act by itself. Each corps had a Light Cav-

alry Division; but in Grouchy's force, the Cavalry Division (Domon's) belonging to Vandamme's Corps, with its horse battery, had been detached to the left wing. Gérard's Corps had its complete parts, but the Seventh Cavalry Division attached to it numbered only 758 men; little more than a modern regiment. The Reserve Cavalry Division, under Jacquinot, also attached to Gérard's Corps, numbered 1608 men, so that the two together would only make a modern brigade. In artillery, the corps, for those days, were well provided; and each corps also had its own engineers, from 140 to 200 strong.

3. *Pursuits after a Battle.*—A general who wins a battle must make every effort to obtain the greatest possible advantages from his victory; he must closely pursue the defeated enemy with cavalry, artillery, and infantry; he must spare no one until the retreat has been turned into a rout. Of the two sides, the vanquished are the more exhausted; and the effects of defeat are so demoralising that, when followed by pursuit, every vestige of organisation or power of resisting vanishes. Men whose backs are turned on a victorious enemy who is treading on their heels, harassing their flanks, and cutting them down or capturing them by thousands, will think of nothing but their personal safety. The more time that is left to the retreating force, the more rear-guard positions it will be able to take up, and every rear-guard action gives time for the retreat to be carried further and in greater security. A timid pursuit is almost worse than none. Every nerve must be strained to make the most of the situation.

Yet, in history, how many instances are there in which pursuits have been carried out? What are the reasons which account for so many battles ending without a pursuit? There are few instances, indeed, where it has been possible for the victor to follow up his victory as is advised in the books. To mention the most noted cases:—The pursuit of the French after Waterloo; the pursuit after Jena; the cavalry advance on Cairo after Tel-el-Kebir; and, most recently, the battles of the Yalu and at Telissu, in the Russo-Japanese War. But how easy it is to recall cases where pursuit has not followed the victory:—Wagram, Friedland, Vittoria, Cannae; Malplaquet, Albuera, Spicheren, Bull Run, and the case treated in this volume, among scores of others.

Many Generals have failed to take the opportunity when it was offered; Hannibal himself was one of them. But in most of the cases there have been strong reasons for the hesitation in pursuing. After a long and fiercely-contested battle, both sides are exhausted; and there may be no fresh troops at hand to carry out the pursuit. There may be heavy rains, making the road impassable; there may be a lack of mounted troops. Most of Wellington's victories in the Peninsular War were so dearly bought that his troops were far too exhausted themselves to think of pursuing the enemy. After Malplaquet Marlborough's army was in no condition to follow up the victory, and the French were able to retreat in fair order and unmolested.

After Spicheren, the Prussians were too exhausted to pursue, and the French withdrew in security. But after Ligny Napoleon should have pursued, at least at daybreak on the 17th. It has been shown that he had a strong force of cavalry, as well as Lobau's Corps, available for the pursuit, and with these he could have driven Thielemann from Sombreffe. His cavalry would have threatened the Prussian Hanks and rear, while Lobau's infantry would have attacked in front.

During the night it was perhaps unwise and unsafe to pursue, owing to Thielemann's firm front, and to the enormous risks of a pursuit by night. No one knew better than Napoleon the value of pressing hard on a vanquished foe, and it is impossible to explain why he spent the morning of the 17th in trividlities. A day later, and he himself realised the position of a defeated general closely and mercilessly pursued by the victors.

Grouchy cannot be blamed, for failing to pursue the Prussians on the, night of the 16th. He was directly under, the Emperor's orders, and he only received his independent command on the morning of the, 17th. At 11 p.m., on the night of the 16th, he had been ordered to send Pajol and Excelmans in pursuit of the Prussians at daybreak, but no direction was given to him. And when it was found that Thielemann's men still held Sombreffe, the cavalry took no further action that night.

Blucher, on the 18th, found it possible to pursue the French with the utmost vigour by night; but there was this difference between the two cases—the French were totally defeated in battle, and demoralised, while the Prussians, at Ligny, were only partially defeated, and their left wing was firm and unbeaten.

It was on the 17th that Grouchy's mistakes began, after he had received his new command from Napoleon, at 11 a.m.

4.—It is astonishing that the outposts of Grouchy's force in front of Sombreffe should have heard nothing, or reported nothing, of Thielemann's withdrawal, which began at 2 a.m., and continued until 4 a.m., when the rear-guard left the village. Throughout the night, the opposing sentries were within earshot; and if they were awake they could not have helped hearing the commotion which must be caused by the movement of so large a body of troops by night, however great the precautions may be.

True, it was a wet night; rain was falling heavily, but not too heavily to drown the noise of the retreat. Even a perfectly-planned and well-executed attack by night, with all the signs predetermined, and each movement marked beforehand, cannot be kept absolutely quiet; there is always a stumbling, a cry of pain from a sprained ankle or broken nose, a curse from the darkness, often a rifle accidentally discharged; but in a retreat hastily decided on, how much greater will the noise be! The shouting of orders which cannot be conveyed by signs or signals on the spur of the moment, the noise of the heavy wagons, the yells of the drivers, and the cracking of whips! In those days the outpost positions would be scarcely two hundred yards apart on such an occasion; very different to modern conditions, which would make it impossible for two forces to remain in the same positions, relative to one another, as Thielemann's and Grouchy's on that night.

5.—Excelmans lacked the true instinct of a cavalry leader. When he found Thielemann at Gembloux, at 9.30 a.m. on the 17th, the first step we should expect him to take would be to send back immediate word to Grouchy; then he would act according to his instructions, or as his own notions prompted. In the present circum-stances, he would have taken steps to harass the enemy, deceive him as to his real numbers, threaten his line of retreat, and force him to march off again, and so spoil his rest and increase the fatigue of his troops, who would soon become too tired either to march or fight, when their retreat would have rapidly become a headlong rout; or to detain him in uncertainty until the infantry arrived.

Certainly, entire inactivity was wrong in such a case. Every hour of rest allowed to Thielemann meant that his troops would be able to march more rapidly when they took the road again. If Thielemann had seen a few squadrons threatening his retreat, a few showing themselves on his flanks, without knowing the real strength of the force overtaking him, it is not conceivable that he would have waited to be attacked by overwhelming numbers.

6.—It must have disconcerted Napoleon to hear Grouchy expostulating as to the orders which he had just given him. The Napoleon of earlier days would have dealt with a heavy hand on the man who dared discuss his orders. No doubt Grouchy felt very strongly on the subject, and his views may very well have been sound—in fact, they were sound up to a certain point; but it is never a soldier's duty to discuss or argue about his orders. The story of Grouchy's insubordination—for insubordination it certainly was—would be difficult to credit, but that some of the best authorities on the campaign give it in their works; and Grouchy himself, in his *Relation Succincte*, openly admits that he made no attempt, in his conversation with the Emperor, to conceal his misgivings.

7.—The mismanagement of the places of assembly and the times of starting the march of different bodies of troops which have to take the same road, leads to miserable confusion. In the present case, there were two Corps d'Armée, Gérard's and Vandamme's, which were required to march from Ligny and St Amand La Haye respectively, to Point-du-Jour by one and the same road. It seems obvious that, time being important, and considering the positions of the two Corps, Gérard's Corps should be marched off first, while Vandamme's should follow as soon as it was ready. But Grouchy, for no reason which can be found, ordered Vandamme to take the lead. Gérard had to wait over one hour while Vandamme's Corps passed him.

It is not an easy matter to arrange, in a case of this kind, that the front corps should be clear by the time that the head of the corps in rear comes up; but Gérard's Corps was sufficiently fax ahead of Vandamme's to allow plenty of time for his men to get on their way before the latter approached, and, at all events, it would have been better to halt Vandamme, while Gérard moved well on the road, than to keep Gérard waiting while Vandamme passed him.

8.—Vandamme's march on Gembloux was extremely slow. He left his bivouac at 12 noon, and arrived at Point-du-Jour, less than four miles off, at 3 p.m., and at Gembloux, another five miles, at 7 p.m. The roads, it must be remembered, were in a deplorable condition, and the rain was falling steadily; but the rate of marching, when compared with the rate of the Prussians over the same road, in only slightly better condition of surface, and with the rate in Grouchy's subsequent retreat, also in heavy weather, is extraordinarily slow.

The guns were moved with great difficulty, and it must be supposed that infantry in large numbers were used to drag them along, but there were still horses to be used, and the Prussians had moved all their guns and wagons successfully. The state of the weather has always been urged in extenuation of Grouchy's slowness in this campaign, but it has been laboured too much. It certainly was a very heavy factor against him, but not so overpowering as is alleged.

9.—Grouchy wasted valuable time in bivouacking at Gembloux, when there were still two hours of daylight left. His men must have been tired with their exertions through the mud; but they had not made extraordinary efforts. French soldiers had proved them-selves capable of greater things in other days, and under other commanders. Had they even pushed on to Sauvenière that night, they would have arrived early enough to allow themselves some six or eight hours rest; or even longer if the cavalry were used with skill. The difficulties of this particular march are often exaggerated; compare it with the marching of the same men two days later, over the same roads, and after continuous fighting for several hours; compare it, too, with some of the marches in the Peninsula, a few years before!

10.—Grouchy's despatch from Gembloux on the night of the 17th to the Emperor cannot be read without a feeling of surprise at his words. In the first place, he says, "My cavalry is at Sauvenière." Now, Napoleon would naturally infer that Pajol's cavalry were included; or that all the cavalry were probably together. It was misleading to say that his "cavalry was at Sauvenière." Secondly, "They (the Prussians) were still here at ten o'clock this morning." The Emperor would at once conclude that the enemy had left soon after ten o'clock; he certainly would suppose that Grouchy would have found out if they had remained there later. Actually, the Prussians left at 2 p.m., four hours later. Thirdly, "He (Blucher) has not passed by Gembloux."

Napoleon would suppose (since Grouchy had been instructed to keep touch with the left wing) that traces of Blucher and his main body had been searched for between the line of Grouchy's march and the main French army. On these three essential points, the information given in the despatch was decidedly misleading. Some other details were inaccurate, but they were reasonable convictions, as far as Grouchy's views went. Negative information in war is very often as useful and important as positive; and Grouchy would have assisted Napoleon to form his ideas if he had reported that he had discovered no signs of a Prussian retreat on Namur.

He should also have made some mention of Pajol's detachment—such as "no news has been received from Pajol, who is on my right at St Denis, with a detachment of cavalry and infantry." Again, had Grouchy only accounted for 80,000 Prussians, of the whole of Blucher's army? What had become of the remainder? Where were they?

Napoleon must have found it impossible to draw inferences of any weight from this despatch; and in such a campaign as this, full and accurate intelligence was of the utmost importance.

11.—A flank march in presence of the enemy is a most difficult and dangerous operation. In the case of Blucher's movement, there was little actual danger from Grouchy, as events proved, but in face of a vigorous enemy the Prussians would have been in a perilous position. It was possible for an active enemy to seize the bridges over the Dyle at Moustier and Ottignies, and fall upon Blucher s flank. The latter was not exposing his communications, for his real communications were with Liège; he had temporarily abandoned them when he marched on Wavre; but if attacked during his march his position would not have been by any means safe. If defeated, whither would he have fallen back? This is the chief danger of a flank march: the lack of a good, or even of any, line of retreat.

As a rule, a flank march, being away from the general line of advance or retreat, has necessarily to be made on lesser roads, and the difficulty of ample movement from one to another, or of rapid deployment or change of front, becomes prodigious. Blucher, if attacked during this march, would most probably have left one corps to detain the enemy, while he, with the other three corps, resumed his march towards Wellington; for to turn back would have been as dangerous as to advance. But if his way had been barred he would have fallen back on Brussels rather than upon Louvain, as he would still have a chance of joining Wellington. If Blucher had been so attacked and defeated, Grouchy would have been able to deal a terrible, in all probability a crushing, blow on Wellington's left flank.

It is interesting, but not particularly profitable, to speculate as to what course events would have taken had Grouchy been up in time to prevent Blucher's flank march, and had checked him. Would Wellington have fallen back on Brussels with Blucher, and fought again under the city walls against Napoleon and Grouchy combined? In that case, the weight of numbers would have been very much in favour of the allies, and the great object of Napoleon's plan of campaign—to prevent the junction of the two armies—would have been thwarted.

If Blucher, after being checked, had fallen back on Louvain, while Wellington was still engaged with Napoleon, it seems obvious that Grouchy's extra numbers thrown into the fight would have caused the Duke's overthrow, for it would not then have been necessary for

Napoleon to detach against the Prussians; Wellington was too seriously engaged to be able to withdraw, and the defeat would have been complete. But after all, such speculation as this might be continued indefinitely; and every campaign might be discussed and argued to a hundred different conclusions by remodelling the conditions or improvising situations. A campaign, like a chess problem, admits of more than one solution.

12. *Grouchy's Retreat.*—A few points concerning Grouchy's retreat may be discussed briefly. Firstly, could he have been intercepted before he reached Namur? The answer is Yes, by Pirch I. Pirch had received orders, on the night of the 18th, to cut off Grouchy from the Sambre; and he had accordingly marched towards Namur through Maransart. He reached Mellery at 11 a.m. on the 19th. At this hour, Grouchy had not begun his retreat. But Pirch's men were tired, and they were halted at Mellery. Had they pushed on another six miles to Gembloux, which they would have reached at 2 p.m., Grouchy's retreat on Namur would have been intercepted.

It is true that Grouchy's force would have greatly outnumbered Pirch's, but the former would not stop to engage the Prussians at Gembloux while Thielemann pressed close on his heels. He would have been forced to make a very wide detour, and in the meantime the Prussians could have hastened on and captured Namur.

Secondly, after Namur, why was not Grouchy more closely pursued? It would have been an idle move to detach a force to follow Grouchy while the advance on Paris was of such immediate importance. At best, Grouchy could threaten the Prussian flank; but he would be more likely to endeavour to join with the remnants of Napoleon's army collected by Soult. Little harm could be done by these forces; and the contagion of defeat might have spread from Soult's fugitives and demoralised Grouchy's men. In any case, the other allied armies were approaching the frontier, and these would be able to deal with Grouchy. The important move was to march on Paris, where the populace, sickened by Napoleon's collapse, were likely to accept terms.

Thirdly, could Grouchy really hope to effect anything advantageous by his retreat on Paris? No, unless he saw a chance of persuading Napoleon to put himself at the head of his troops and the Paris garrison, and march out to repeat the strokes of 1814; but on the 22nd Napoleon had abdicated.

Fourthly, could he have effected more by marching south to rally Suchet and Lecourbe? Hardly; since overwhelming armies were approaching on that side, and the fall of Paris would render resistance in the country districts useless.

His case was really hopeless from the first. The allies in their march on Paris would ignore him, and, moving by a much more direct road, would reach the capital first. The triple line of fortresses across the line of advance of the enemy, were expected to bar his approach, but they were weakly garrisoned by ill-disciplined and raw troops, whose whole spirit was shaken by Napoleon's great defeat.

So far-reaching is the effect of a defeat as great as Waterloo that armies, districts, even capitals, miles from the real theatre of war, possibly in other countries, seem to crumble to dust before the conqueror; but no fall from might and power has ever been so great as Napoleon's.

Marshal Grouchy's Report Addressed to the Emperor
BY MARSHAL DE GROUCHY.

¹Dinant, June 20th, 1815.—It was not till after seven in the evening of the 18th of June, that I received the letter of the Duke of Dalmatia, which directed me to march on St Lambert, and to attack General Bulow. I fell in with the enemy as I was marching on Wavre. He was immediately driven into Wavre, and General Vandamme's corps attacked that town, and was warmly engaged. The portion of Wavre, on the right of the Dyle, was carried, but much difficulty was experienced in debouching on the other side. General Girard was wounded by a ball in the breast while endeavouring to carry the mill of Bielge, in order to pass the river, but in which he did not succeed, and Lieutenant-General Aix had been killed in the attack on the town.

In this state of things, being impatient to co-operate with your Majesty's army on that important day, I detached several corps to force the passage of the Dyle and march against Bulow. The corps of Vandamme, in the meantime, maintained the attack on Wavre, and on the mill, whence the enemy showed an intention to debouch, but which I did not conceive he was capable of effecting. I arrived at Limale, passed the river, and the heights were carried by the division of Vichery and the cavalry. Night did not permit us to advance farther, and I no longer heard the cannon on the side where your Majesty was engaged.

I halted in this situation until daylight. Wavre and Bielge were occupied by the Prussians, who, at three in the morning of the 18th, attacked in their turn, wishing to take advantage of the difficult position

---

1. Extract from *The Journal of the Three Days of the Battle of Waterloo* by An Eyewitness.

in which I was, and expecting to drive me into the defile, and take the artillery which had debouched, and make me repass the Dyle. Their efforts were fruitless. The Prussians were repulsed, and the village of Bielge taken. The brave General Penny was killed.

General Vandamme then passed one of his divisions by Bielge, and carried with ease the heights of Wavre, and along the whole of my line the success was complete. I was in front of Rozierne, preparing to march on Brussels, when I received the sad intelligence of the loss of the Battle of Waterloo. The officer who brought it informed me, that your Majesty was retreating on the Sambre, without being able to indicate any particular point on which I should direct my march. I ceased to pursue, and began my retrograde movement. The retreating enemy did not think of following me.

Learning that the enemy had already passed the Sambre, and was on my flank, and not being sufficiently strong to make a diversion in favour of your Majesty, without compromising that which I commanded, I marched on Namur. At this moment, the rear of the columns were attacked. That of the left made a retrograde movement sooner than was expected, which endangered, for a moment, the retreat of the left; but good dispositions soon repaired everything, and two pieces which had been, taken were recovered by the brave 20th Dragoons, who besides took an howitzer from the enemy.

We entered Namur without loss. The long defile which extends from this place to Dinant, in which only a single column can march, and the embarrassment arising from the numerous transports of wounded rendered: it necessary to hold for a considerable time the town, in which I had not the means of blowing up the bridge. I entrusted the defence of Namur to General Vandamme, who, with his usual intrepidity maintained himself there till eight in the evening; so that nothing was left behind, and I occupied Dinant

The enemy has lost some thousands of men in the attack on Namur, where the contest was very obstinate; the troops, have performed their duty in a manner worthy of praise.

 (Signed)   De Grouchy.

Marshal Grouchy's Force

THIRD CORPS—Vandamme.

Eighth Division—(Lefol)

	Battns.	Men.
15th Light Infantry, 23rd, 37th, and 64th Regiments of the Line	11	
Tenth Division—(Habert)		
22nd, 34th, 70th and 88th Regiments of the Line	12	14,508
Eleventh Division—(Berthézène)		
12th, 33rd, 56th, and 86th Regiments of the Line	8	
Battalions Infantry	31	

Artillery

	Men.	Guns.
4 batteries Foot [1] Artillery (8 guns each)	782	32
Engineers	146	

---

[1] The French foot batteries contained 8 guns; the horse batteries, 6 guns. The horse battery belonging to Vandamme's Corps had been detached with Domon's Light Cavalry Division, to the Left Wing.

TOTALS, THIRD CORPS

Infantry	14,508
Artillery	782, 32 guns.
Engineers	146
	15,536 men.

FOURTH CORPS—Gérard.
   Twelfth Division—(Pecheux)
      30th, 63rd, and 96th Regiments of   Battns.   Men.
        the Line . . . . . 10⎫
   Thirteenth Division—(Vichery)   ⎪
      48th, 59th, 69th, and 76th Regi-   ⎬ 12,589
        ments of the Line . . . 8   ⎪
   Fourteenth Division—(Hulot)   ⎪
      9th Light Infantry, 44th, 50th, and   ⎭
        111th Regiments of the Line . 8

            Battalions Infantry . . 26

   Seventh Cavalry Division—(Maurin)   Squadrons. Men.
      6th Hussars . . . . . 3⎫
                       ⎬ 758
      8th Chasseurs . . . . 3⎭

   Reserve Cavalry Division—(Jacquinot)
      6th, 11th, 15th, and 16th Dragoons 16   1,608

   Artillery   Guns.
      4 Batteries Foot Artillery . . 32⎫
                             ⎬ 1,538
      1 Battery Horse Artillery . . 6⎭

   Engineers 201

        TOTALS, FOURTH CORPS

   Infantry . . . . . . 12,589 men.
   Cavalry . . . . . . 2,366 ,,
   Artillery . . . . . . 1,538 ,,
   Engineers . . . . . . 201 ,,

       Total . . . . 16,694 ,, 38 guns

TWENTY-FIRST DIVISION—Teste. Detached from Lobau's Corps.
   8th Light Infantry, 40th, 65th, and 75th   Battns. Men.
      Regiments of the Line . . . 5   2,316

Artillery attached to the Division—   Guns.
   1 Battery Foot Artillery . . . 8   161

      Total, Teste's Division . 2,477 men, 8 guns.

Cavalry

FOURTH CAVALRY DIVISION (belonging to 1st Cavalry Corps) under PAJOL (commanding First Cavalry Corps)—

	Squadrons.	Men.
1st, 4th, and 5th Hussars	12	1,234

Artillery attached to this Cavalry Division—

	Guns.	Men.
1 Battery Horse Artillery	6	154

SECOND CAVALRY CORPS (EXCELMANS')—

Ninth Cavalry Division—(Strolz)   Squadrons.
5th, 13th, 15th, and 20th Dragoons 16 ⎫
Tenth Cavalry Division (Chastel)   ⎬ 2,817
4th, 12th, 14th, and 17th Dragoons 15 ⎭

Artillery attached to the Second Cavalry Corps—

	Guns.	
2 Batteries Horse Artillery	12	246

SUMMARY OF GROUCHY'S FORCES.

	Infantry.	Cavalry.	Artillery.	Engrs.	Guns.
Third Corps, Vandamme	14,508	—	782	146	32
Fourth Corps, Gérard	12,589	2,366	1,538	201	38
Twenty-First Division, Teste	2,316	—	161	—	8
Fourth Cav. Division, Pajol	—	1,234	154	—	6
Second Cav. Corps, Excelmans'	—	2,817	246	—	12
	29,413	6,417	2,881	347	96
Deducting losses at Ligny	3,940	907	600	—	—
TOTALS	25,473	5,510	2,281	347	96

33,611 men, 96 guns.

ALSO FROM LEONAUR
AVAILABLE IN SOFTCOVER OR HARDCOVER WITH DUST JACKET

IRON TIMES WITH THE GUARDS by An O. E. (G. P. A. Fildes)—The Experiences of an Officer of the Coldstream Guards on the Western Front During the First World War.

THE GREAT WAR IN THE MIDDLE EAST: 1 by W. T. Massey—The Desert Campaigns & How Jerusalem Was Won---two classic accounts in one volume.

THE GREAT WAR IN THE MIDDLE EAST: 2 by W. T. Massey—Allenby's Final Triumph.

SMITH-DORRIEN by Horace Smith-Dorrien—Isandlwhana to the Great War.

1914 by Sir John French—The Early Campaigns of the Great War by the British Commander.

CAVALRY AT WATERLOO by Sir Evelyn Wood—British Mounted Troops During the Campaign of 1815.

THE SUBALTERN by George Robert Gleig—The Experiences of an Officer of the 85th Light Infantry During the Peninsular War.

DIGGERS AT WAR by R. Hugh Knyvett & G. P. Cuttriss—"Over There" With the Australians by R. Hugh Knyvett and Over the Top With the Third Australian Division by G. P. Cuttriss. Accounts of Australians During the Great War in the Middle East, at Gallipoli and on the Western Front.

THE LIGHT INFANTRY OFFICER by John H. Cooke—The Experiences of an Officer of the 43rd Light Infantry in America During the War of 1812.

THE CAMELIERS by Oliver Hogue—A Classic Account of the Australians of the Imperial Camel Corps During the First World War in the Middle East.

RED DUST by Donald Black—A Classic Account of Australian Light Horsemen in Palestine During the First World War.

NAPOLEON AT BAY, 1814 by F. Loraine Petre—The Campaigns to the Fall of the First Empire.

NAPOLEON AND THE CAMPAIGN OF 1806 by Colonel Vachée—The Napoleonic Method of Organisation and Command to the Battles of Jena & Auerstädt.

THE COMPLETE ADVENTURES IN THE CONNAUGHT RANGERS by William Grattan—The 88th Regiment during the Napoleonic Wars by a Serving Officer.

AVAILABLE ONLINE AT www.leonaur.com
AND FROM ALL GOOD BOOK STORES

ALSO FROM LEONAUR
AVAILABLE IN SOFTCOVER OR HARDCOVER WITH DUST JACKET

FARAWAY CAMPAIGN *by F. James*—Experiences of an Indian Army Cavalry Officer in Persia & Russia During the Great War.

REVOLT IN THE DESERT *by T. E. Lawrence*—An account of the experiences of one remarkable British officer's war from his own perspective.

MACHINE-GUN SQUADRON *by A. M. G.*—The 20th Machine Gunners from British Yeomanry Regiments in the Middle East Campaign of the First World War.

A GUNNER'S CRUSADE *by Antony Bluett*—The Campaign in the Desert, Palestine & Syria as Experienced by the Honourable Artillery Company During the Great War.

DESPATCH RIDER *by W. H. L. Watson*—The Experiences of a British Army Motorcycle Despatch Rider During the Opening Battles of the Great War in Europe.

TIGERS ALONG THE TIGRIS *by E. J. Thompson*—The Leicestershire Regiment in Mesopotamia During the First World War.

HEARTS & DRAGONS *by Charles R. M. F. Crutwell*—The 4th Royal Berkshire Regiment in France and Italy During the Great War, 1914-1918.

INFANTRY BRIGADE: 1914 *by John Ward*—The Diary of a Commander of the 15th Infantry Brigade, 5th Division, British Army, During the Retreat from Mons.

NAPOLEONIC WAR STORIES *by Sir Arthur Quiller-Couch*—Tales of soldiers, spies, battles & sieges from the Peninsular & Waterloo campaingns.

CAPTAIN OF THE 95TH (RIFLES) *by Jonathan Leach*—An officer of Wellington's sharpshooters during the Peninsular, South of France and Waterloo campaigns of the Napoleonic wars.

RIFLEMAN COSTELLO *by Edward Costello*—The adventures of a soldier of the 95th (Rifles) in the Peninsular & Waterloo Campaigns of the Napoleonic wars.

RIFLEMAN MACGILL'S WAR *by Patrick MacGill*—A Soldier of the London Irish During the Great War in Europe including *The Amateur Army*, *The Red Horizon* & *The Great Push*.

WITH THE GUNS *by C. A. Rose & Hugh Dalton*—Two First Hand Accounts of British Gunners at War in Europe During World War 1- Three Years in France with the Guns and With the British Guns in Italy.

THE BUSH WAR DOCTOR *by Robert V. Dolbey*—The Experiences of a British Army Doctor During the East African Campaign of the First World War.

AVAILABLE ONLINE AT **www.leonaur.com**
AND FROM ALL GOOD BOOK STORES

www.ingramcontent.com/pod-product-compliance
Lightning Source LLC
Chambersburg PA
CBHW021010090426
42738CB00007B/733